YO-BPW-288

THE GOOD APPLE CREATIVE WRITING BOOK BY:

# GARY GRIMM
# DON MITCHELL

ILLUSTRATED BY:

## Gary Grimm

Published by

Good Apple, Inc.
299 Jefferson Road
P.O. Box 480
Parsippany, NJ 07054-0480

ISBN No. 0-916456-04-8

Copyright 1976 by Good Apple, Inc.

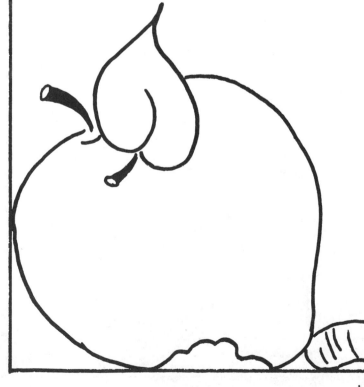

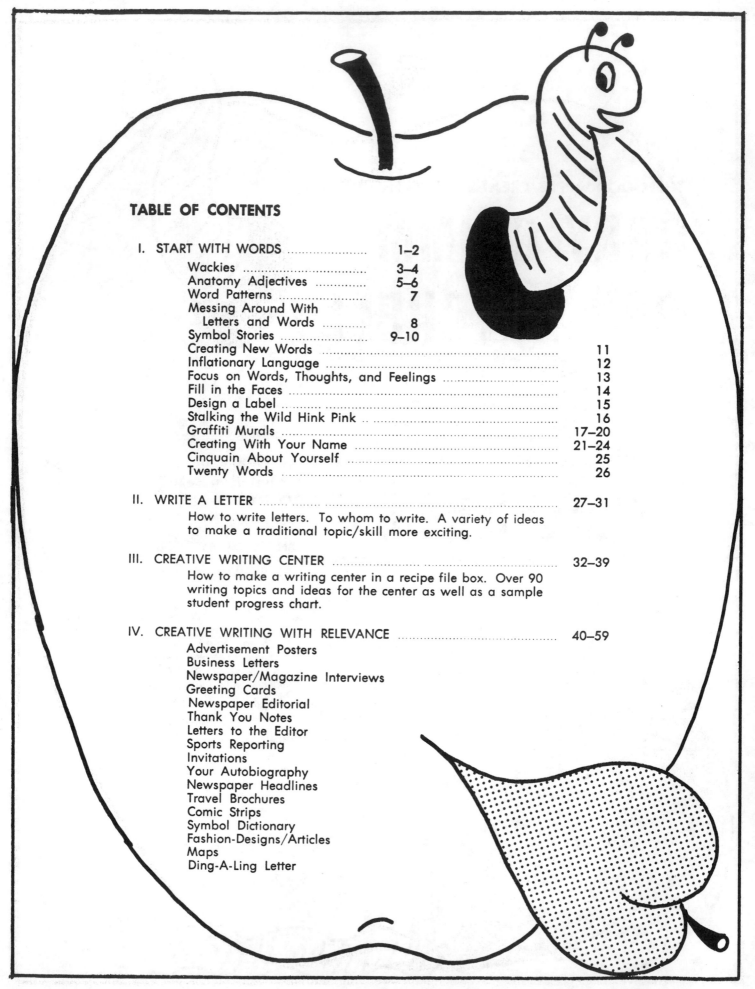

# TABLE OF CONTENTS

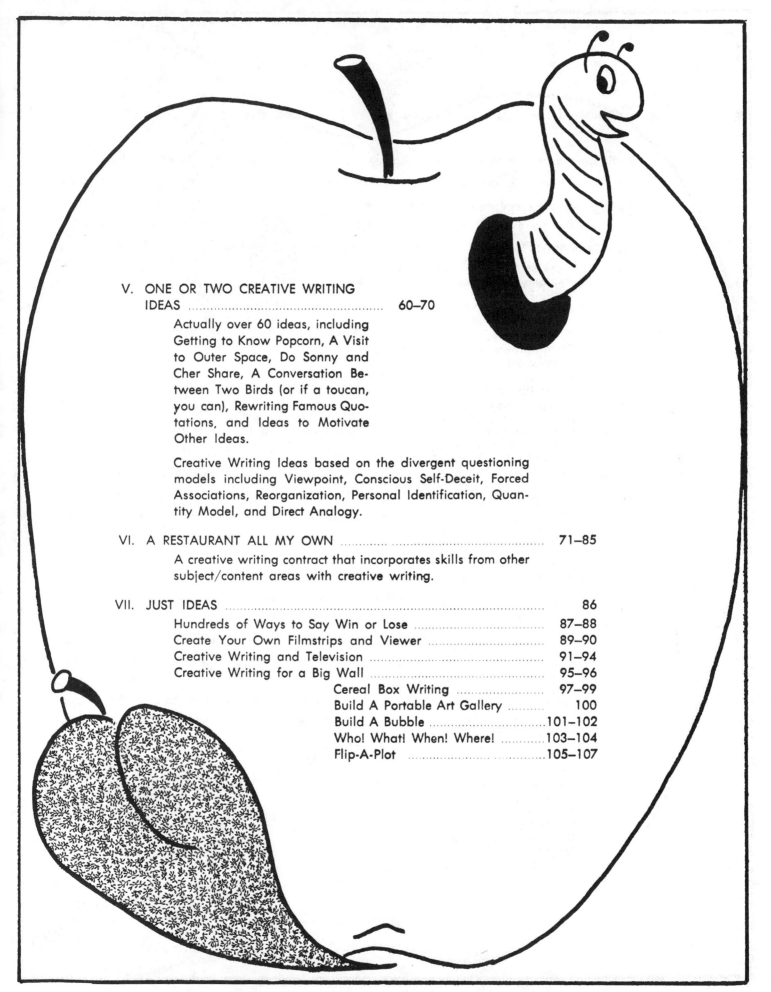

## We Have Published the Good Apple Creative Writing Book Because . . . . . .

Many materials on the market today ignore the talent of students who possess originality of thinking and inventiveness. These materials focus on convergent thinking (coming up with one and only one correct answer). Although we at Good Apple agree students must be taught the skills of inquiry and research, we feel they must also have the opportunity to work with materials that will expand their creative thinking and writing abilities. We would like to give creative thinking and writing the attention it deserves.

This book will focus on divergent and evaluative thinking skills. We believe these two thinking abilities realistically help students prepare for the demands of our changing future. We also realize that many of our daily decisions are based on the divergency and evaluation of our memorized facts and skills. Someone may ask, "Why have you used this particular format and approach?"

Our basic philosophy has always been to provide teachers with practical, easy-to-use ideas at a reasonable price. This is the approach that has been successful in our Good Apple Newspaper and this is the approach we are using in our books. Most activities found in this book are ready to use as they are and many of the activities can be used directly by students. Several different approaches have been used to accommodate various learning styles. When we developed this book we tried to focus more on the process and not so much on the product. The activities found in this creative writing book will allow students opportunities to play around with all kinds of possibilities. Activities that tickle the students' imagination.

One important part of this creative writing book is to provide relevant alternatives. Alternatives allow students the flexibility to choose an area of interest and the opportunity to assume some responsibility for the development of their creative writing skills. By working with alternatives such as advertisements, symbol messages, comic strips, menus, and want ads, the creative writing topics are focused upon contemporary interest and usable skills and concepts. We believe this is one giant step toward relevancy.

We feel we have compiled a collection of teacher-tested creative writing ideas that can be the gateway to discovery of divergency and imagination for thousands of boys and girls. We hope you enjoy your new book and wish the best of luck to you and your students.

Gary and Don

# Creating A Proper Classroom Climate for Creative Writing

## What Does Your Classroom Climate Say?

If you were to assume the role of one of your students, to sit quietly at a desk in the middle of your classroom, what would you discover about your classroom climate? What would you see when you look at the room you and your students occupy for nine months? Would you see color? Is it cluttered? Is it neat? Does everything have its place? Do you see an environment conducive to the development of creativity? How does the climate of your room make you feel — insignificant — small — large — afraid — confused — self-conscious? What do you hear? What kinds of questions do you hear being asked verbally and what kinds do you see on daily assignments and written tests? Is your room warm, cold, light or dark? If asked, could you tell someone what your classroom climate says? Does the climate of your classroom and your school support the development of the creative abilities of your students?

## What Is A Good Climate?

The classroom climate that develops creative thinkers and writers will be one that supports the development of skills in discovering analogies, similies, metaphors and the juxtaposition or forced association of facts and ideas that might not at first appear to be interrelated. One that provides open-ended questions asking students to be fluent, flexible, original and to elaborate on both their own and the ideas of others. This climate will be alive with ideas, color, materials and will provide the all important positive support.

## A Good Climate Supports Students

A good climate says that it's all right to be yourself, to be spontaneous. One in which novel ideas and unconventional thoughts and actions are widely tolerated and not overly criticized. A climate that gives precedence to expressions of thoughts, feelings and emotions over mechanics and form. A climate that stresses caring and sharing as much as spelling and neatness. A climate that says it's okay to take a chance; a climate that cries out, **"Dare to be different."** A climate that will not only encourage a student's divergence, but will attempt to help him understand and communicate that difference.

## A Good Climate Will Show Students How To Evaluate

A climate that fosters creative thinking will be one where students and teacher work together to accomplish mutual goals. A climate where both teacher and students can learn to suspend judgment temporarily to avoid undue interruption in their thinking. After ideas have accumulated, they can formulate criteria for judging and making decisions. A climate where true evaluation comes from within and grades, if required, are the expected verification of proof required by parents and grandparents.

## A Good Climate Allows Courage To Develop

A student with creative potential must have the courage to be different in thought and action; the courage to stand out and if necessary to be in conflict with teachers and peers. A few students with creative abilities come to school possessing this courage — most do not, and it's our job as teachers to not only ask the divergent and evaluative questions, to provide the stimulating materials and physical surrounding, but also to provide a climate that is psychologically safe. Yes, it's your job, teacher, to create the climate. Your verbal and non-verbal behavior must present a model that will allow each potentially creative student under your guidance the opportunity to find the courage to be different and allow the spirit of creativity the opportunity to flourish. Yes, it's your job, teacher, to create the climate.

lazy

fal_

~DOG~ (sun/dog illustration)

ON TOP OF IT

Mostly Mountainous

# START
# WITH
# WORDS

REFLECT
REEFLECT (mirror reflection)

backwards

Stra......

ARROW.....y (arrow pointing up)

A good place to begin developing creative writing skills in your students is with WORDS. Words can become sentences. Sentences can become paragraphs. Paragraphs can become stories. So the best place to begin may be at the beginning . . . . . . the WORD.

In this section of the book you will find several activities that we feel will help your students think creatively and therefore write creatively with words.

The idea illustrated on this page is an easy one. Can you make a word express its meaning? Can you write the word cold to look cold? Give each student several 3'' x 5'' index cards. On each card they can place a word written so that it expresses its meaning. This can be an on-going project . . . . . . maybe over a two-week period. Each time the student thinks of another example he prints it on a card and then tapes it on the wall of the classroom. The idea will catch on and before long you will have to build a bigger wall, stop the activity, or think of another alternative.

This idea can be turned into a project that can continue throughout the whole school year. As your students complete cards they can be filed in a recipe box that has been titled, Picture Words, or Word Pictures, or Word Power. Each entry should be filed alphabetically. The possibilities for words to include are almost endless . . . shaggy, fluffy, narrow, fancy, balloons, marshmallow, plaid, endless, pink, hot, curly, icicle, ice-cream cone, small, obese, porthole, sailboat, round . . . the list could go on and on. Your students will enjoy thinking creatively. This is also a nice project to use to illustrate the idea that not everyone has to get involved to the same degree. Perhaps everyone should try to do one or two cards. Some students will not wish to do any more. Other students will "turn on" and enjoy completing many cards. This type of involvement should be encouraged and recognized. You will probably have some students who will not get involved at first, but after a couple of months may become very productive.

FURTHER EXTENSION IDEAS: Students could determine when a really good card has been developed and this could be redone on a sheet of 8½'' x 11'' white paper using bright magic markers. All examples done this way could be displayed on classroom or hall walls.

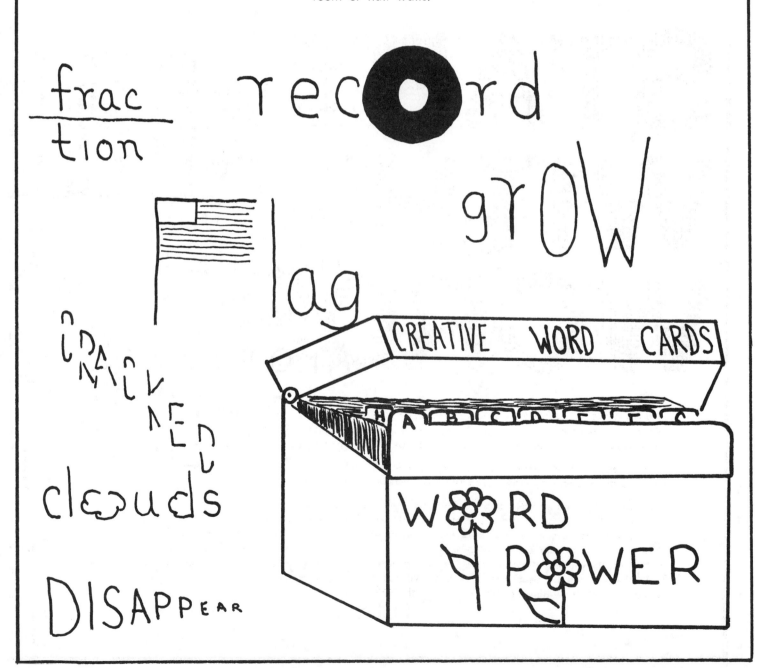

# WACKIES!

engagvement

ONE KIND
ONE KIND
ONE KIND
ONE KIND
ONE KIND
ONE KIND
ANOTHER
ANOTHER
ANOTHER
ANOTHER
ANOTHER
ANOTHER

Can you figure out what the WACKIES !!! on this page say? If you can, you will also understand how to design some. A Hole IN One was easy to figure out wasn't it. You also probably didn't have much trouble with Broken Engagement. The other two are a little harder. They are Six of One Kind, Half a Dozen of Another . . . . and . . . . Misunderstanding Between Friends. The next page gives you the opportunity to figure out some more as well as the opportunity to design some of your own. Have fun.

friends standing friends
miss

| | | |
|---|---|---|
| I I I I I right I I I I I I | | sgeg |
| | eggs eggs<br>EASY | |
| RANGER | | safe<br>first |
| | R<br>G ROSIE I<br>N | |

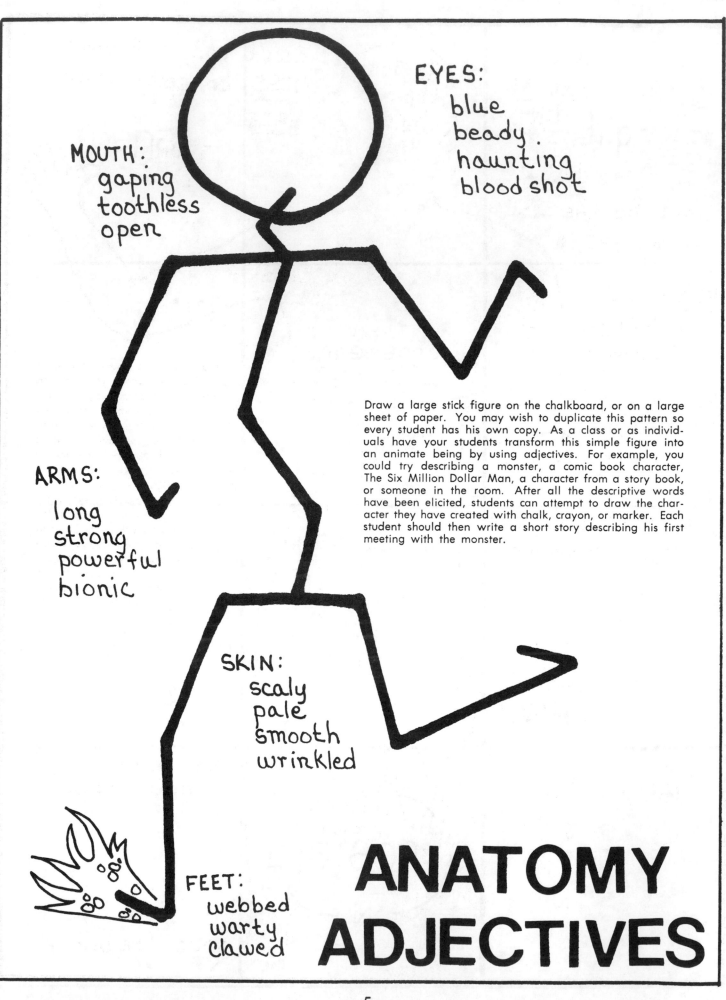

EYES:
blue
beady
haunting
blood shot

MOUTH:
gaping
toothless
open

Draw a large stick figure on the chalkboard, or on a large sheet of paper. You may wish to duplicate this pattern so every student has his own copy. As a class or as individuals have your students transform this simple figure into an animate being by using adjectives. For example, you could try describing a monster, a comic book character, The Six Million Dollar Man, a character from a story book, or someone in the room. After all the descriptive words have been elicited, students can attempt to draw the character they have created with chalk, crayon, or marker. Each student should then write a short story describing his first meeting with the monster.

ARMS:
long
strong
powerful
bionic

SKIN:
scaly
pale
smooth
wrinkled

FEET:
webbed
warty
clawed

# ANATOMY ADJECTIVES

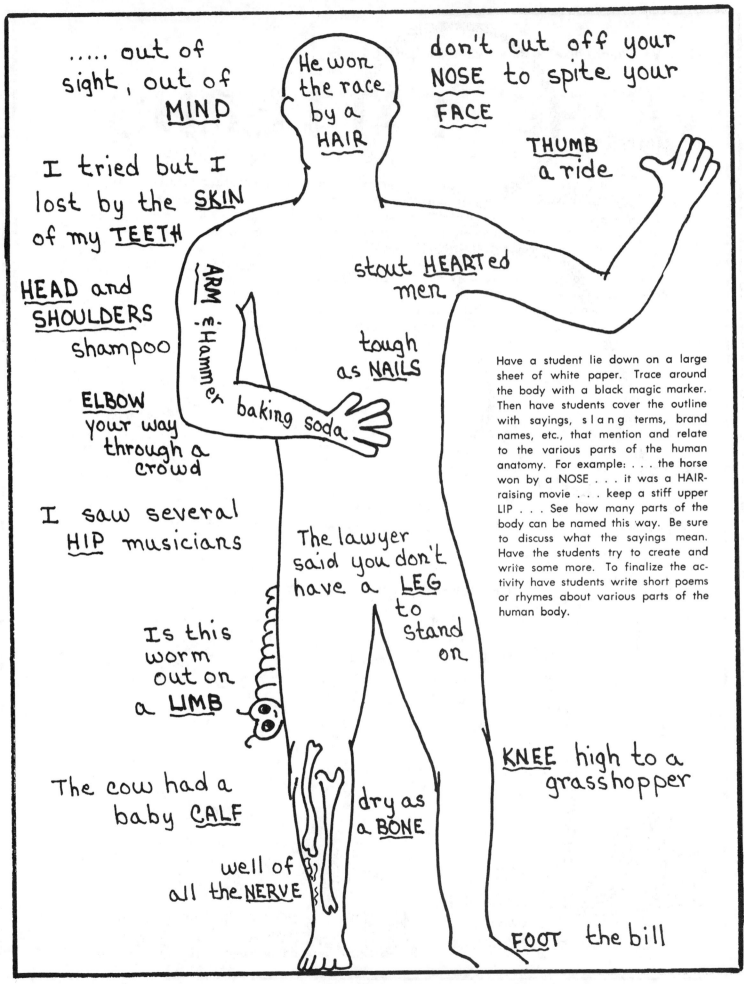

..... out of sight, out of **MIND**

He won the race by a **HAIR**

don't cut off your **NOSE** to spite your **FACE**

**THUMB** a ride

I tried but I lost by the **SKIN** of my **TEETH**

**HEAD** and **SHOULDERS** shampoo

ARM & Hammer

**ELBOW** your way through a crowd

baking soda

stout **HEART**ed men

tough as **NAILS**

I saw several **HIP** musicians

The lawyer said you don't have a **LEG** to stand on

Is this worm out on a **LIMB**

The cow had a baby **CALF**

dry as a **BONE**

**KNEE** high to a grasshopper

well of all the **NERVE**

**FOOT** the bill

Have a student lie down on a large sheet of white paper. Trace around the body with a black magic marker. Then have students cover the outline with sayings, s l a n g terms, brand names, etc., that mention and relate to the various parts of the human anatomy. For example: . . . the horse won by a NOSE . . . it was a HAIR-raising movie . . . keep a stiff upper LIP . . . See how many parts of the body can be named this way. Be sure to discuss what the sayings mean. Have the students try to create and write some more. To finalize the activity have students write short poems or rhymes about various parts of the human body.

# WORD PATTERNS

If you have a typewriter in your classroom, it would be great to use for this project. If not, just by printing, you and your students can begin making a collection of word patterns. Word patterns are words that use their letters to make the shape of the word they represent. The word rectangle is a good example. It would be typed or printed enough times to form a rectangle
rectangle
rectangle.

Before each student begins to work independently, you might like to have a class discussion and brainstorming session. You could use the following words as samples during the large group session: . . . swoop . . . circle . . . square . . . triangle . . . line . . . swerve . . . diamond . . . curve . . . hill . . . uneven . . . downstairs . . . arrow.

A
R
E
H
M
I
L
T
P
F

## MORE MESSING AROUND WITH LETTERS AND WORDS

Given 10 letters of the alphabet (don't forget to include vowels) discover:

    . . . . how many words you can create

    . . . . how many two-letter words, three-letter words, etc.

    . . . . Now, with the words you have created, can you write:

        . . . . a sentence

        . . . . a paragraph

        . . . . a short story

        . . . . a slogan

        . . . . a poem

Of course you can add prepositions and conjunctions.

SENTENCE: Fat Pat hit the flat mat.

Pat lit the match. He hit the mat, flipped the match.
The match hot, the flat not
Fat Pat flipped the mat etc.

| | | | | |
|---|---|---|---|---|
| are | ripe | hear | mile | limp |
| arm | rail | hair | me | learn |
| alter | trail | harm | mean | lean |
| aim | trial | heart | meat | lap |
| ale | tear | hail | melt | let |
| rim | tea | heal | mar | mat |
| rip | tile | he | mire | mit |
| ream | 'til | hit | ma | flip |
| real | time | her | am | lair |
| tie | tire | him | it | pie |
| hi | help | half | ire | pa |
| if | air | tie | lip | pat |
| pet | pit | par | pelt | pear |
| pare | pair | felt | far | fir |
| film | fare | frame | firm | fit |

# the story of LITTLE MISS MUFFET

Some of your students will enjoy this type of creative writing. Symbol writing is fun, challenging and creative. Symbols replace words. Reading the stories can also be creative. Without the words present it is a matter of interpreting exactly what the symbols mean. Many times the plot can become more complicated because visually much more is present.

Have your students choose a nursery rhyme or familiar fairy tale . . . develop symbols for characters and props . . . and create a symbol story.

 LITTLE MISS MUFFET

 TUFFET

SPIDER

CURDS & WHEY

little miss muffet

sat on a tuffet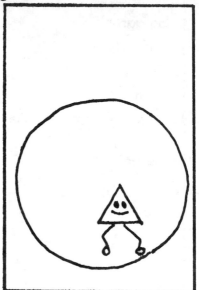

eating curds & whey

along came a spider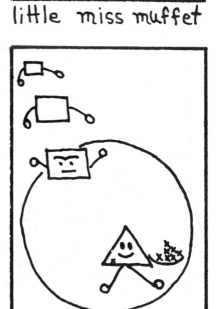

sat down beside her

frightened miss muffet away

One way to have your students illustrate these symbol stories is to give each student several sheets of construction paper. They cut out the symbols from the construction paper and glue them on a background sheet of construction paper of another color. Felt-tip markers can be used to add detail, if needed. Symbol stories, made in this way, are colorful and they can be seen by all students when they are held in front of the class or when they are taped on the classroom wall. Symbol stories present an excellent opportunity for older students to share with primary students. Don't forget to discuss the reactions to the presentations. This is an outstanding opportunity for meaningful evaluation and growth.

Challenge your students to develop nursery rhymes or fairly tales of their own. You may wish to draw boxes on a duplicating master and run several copies for each of your students. The students can then use fine tipped felt pens to draw their symbols in the proper sequence.

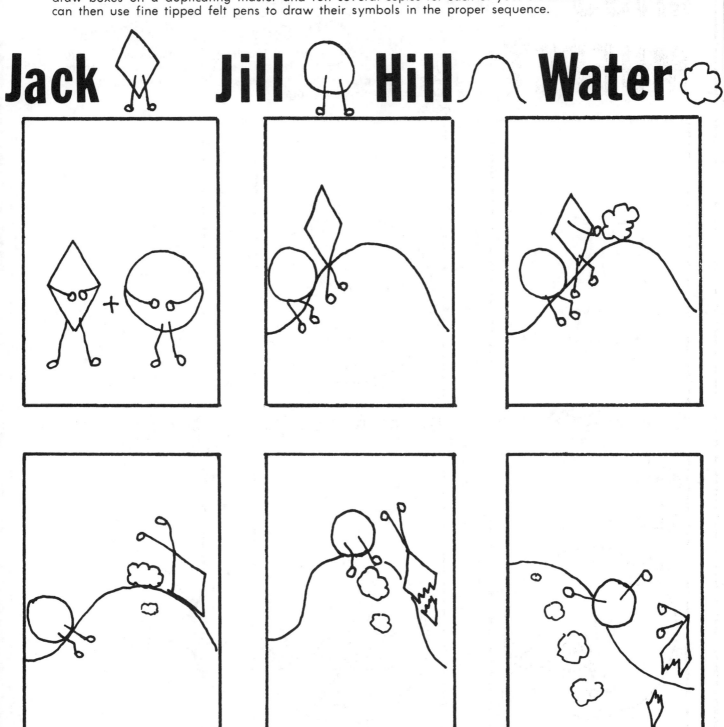

# Creating New Words

Recently a TV weatherman used a couple of strange words during the 10:00 o'clock weather report. He said that in Idaho and Montana they were having SNAIN and SNAIL. The station was flooded with telephone calls and several letters were received demanding to know exactly what snain and snail were. Snain turned out to be a new word meaning snow mixed with rain. Snail was, of course, snow and hail. Two new words were born into a rapidly expanding vocabulary. Seldom do we take the time to really listen and learn new words unless they merit extreme popularity like motel and smog. It wasn't too many years ago that smoke and fog married and along came baby smog. Your students will have fun creating, writing, and defining new words. Words they make up. Who knows, their words might catch on like brunch, heliport, television, stereophonic, or peekapoo. These words aren't really new, at least to a ten-year old . . . it is just us old timers past 25 who can't keep pace with our ever-changing language.

# INFLATIONARY LANGUAGE

Inflation is a growing concern to many of us. Prices keep rising higher and higher. Almost everything is worth more today than it was yesterday. But our language has not adjusted to inflation.

Shouldn't **ten**nis be **eleven**nis?

And Mary Tyler Moore should really be either Mary Tyler Much Moore or Mary Tyler Less.

Before could become befive and even tulips would inflate to threelips.

OK! Now you have the idea. Take words with numbers in them, or homonyms of number words and rewrite them . . . raising each one number.

**Cre**ate = cr**enine**    \*\*\*    Don Juan = Don Two    \*\*\*    canine = caten

Your students can think of as many examples as possible. Develop an inflation dictionary. Write an inflationary letter. Create an inflation story.

Five score and eight years ago our fivefathers set fifth . . . etc.

Twice upon a time . . .

Pretty soon I'll be a trio and not a pear

Words and Thoughts and Feelings Focus on

Any number of words can be used for this exercise . . . but today let's be HAPPY

1. Make a list of all the things that make you happy. Don't evaluate . . . just write down the ideas as you think of them.

2. Write your own definition of the word happy.

3. What words mean just about the same thing as happy? Write down this list of synonyms.

4. Describe how you feel when you are happy.

5. Can a person live happily ever after?

6. Write all the forms of the word happy that you can think of. For example: unhappy, happiness, slap happy.

Use pictures from magazines or pictures you draw to illustrate happy and its forms.

Now choose a word you like . . . it can be a word, a thought, a feeling. Try the same techniques and activities that we used with happy.

# FILL-IN FACES

Fill-in faces are fun. Just complete the facial features to show what the person is doing. The expression you sketch will show how the person feels . . . maybe what his opinion is, or even what is happening. The same face can be completed to show a variety of emotions or reactions. If you design groups of faces they can focus on a topic. Just title each group . . . at the ball game . . . at church . . . while teacher isn't looking . . . After the faces have been completed comes the creative writing activity. Have the faces talk. Students write in "clouds" what the person is thinking or saying. Fill-in faces can help students become better acquainted with their own emotions and non-verbal behavior. This activity will help writing creatively with conversation. Fill-in faces for your students to work with can be developed from your imagination, comic book characters, coloring book people, or faces in magazines. They can be drawn and duplicated or cut out (faceless) and placed under transparent sheets where students draw with a grease pencil and then erase with a tissue.

# Design A Label

Save a variety of tin cans and their labels . . . at least one for every student in your classroom. Bring the cans to class but save the labels. They will be used later. Cut strips of white paper to fit each can and place inside. Then put all the cans in a large box or sack and allow each student to choose one. Their task is to create a label for their can. It can be any kind of product that they feel would come in the style of can they chose. Students can use markers, pens, pencils, crayons, or pictures from magazines to complete their label. The label they create can be for a real product or one they invent. When all are completed, pass out the actual labels for the cans. Have students read the labels and discuss what information the various labels contain. Then give each student a second white paper label. They will do a better job this time. Not only have you provided your students with a creative writing lesson, but also a lesson in consumer education.

# Stalking the Wild HINK PINK

Do you have a wild "HINK-PINK" lurking in your classroom? Perhaps even maybe a "HINKY-PINKY"?
A Hink Pink is a two one-syllable word combination answering a word game riddle. The two one-syllable words must rhyme.
Example: What would you call a plump feline? Answer: FAT CAT.
A HINKY PINKY is a two two-syllable word combination.
Example: What would you call a comical hare? Answer: FUNNY BUNNY.
If some of your students are looking for a real challenge, try a few HINKETY PINKETIES. These, of course, are two three-syllable word combinations. For example: What would you call an awful looking garment? Answer: TERRIBLE WEARABLE.

Here are a few HINK PINKS to get you and your class started

1. colorful jester
2. excellent backbone
3. smart insect
4. artificial goodie
5. impartial animal

6. honest robber
7. different pasture
8. happy parent
9. heated pan
10. terrific territory

1. brown clown
2. fine spine
3. sly fly
4. fake cake
5. fair bear

6. good hood
7. strange range
8. glad dad
9. hot pot
10. great state

HELLO! I'm what's known as your typical, average, wild HINK PINK. Grrrrrr!

And here are some hinky-pinkies:

1. beautiful animal    —    pretty kitty
2. particular girl      —    choosy Suzie
3. inquisitive flower   —    nosey posey
4. sassy longhair       —    snippy hippy
5. questionable woman   —    shady lady

# GRAFFITI MURALS

## The purpose:

1). To allow students the opportunity to express their ideas freely on a variety of topics in a non-threatening way. 2). To allow students the opportunity to expand, elaborate, "piggyback," on the ideas of other students. 3). To provide a lesson that allows all students to contribute successfully. It is hard to write something wrong on a graffiti mural. 4). To allow students the opportunity to make their word a part of the classroom atmosphere. 5). TO PROVIDE IDEAS FOR ADDITIONAL CREATIVE WRITING EFFORTS. The graffiti mural is the divergent thinking part of creative writing. Students can then use the ideas, evaluate them, and write something of quality.

## Some basic rules:

1). Try not to express your "teacher's" opinion . . . at least not until the mural is completed. After completion is a good time for a class discussion focusing on the topic. 2). Provide a lot of encouragement. Encourage the students to express themselves freely, and honestly. 3). Try not to impose your values . . . allow students to discover and learn from each other. 4). You may need to set a couple of basic ground rules like — Everyone must contribute at least once and nothing may be written that makes fun of a classmate.

## Where to & how to:

1). A section of the chalkboard, outlined or framed with construction paper. All you need to supply is chalk . . . colored will make the mural nicer. 2). A sheet of tagboard or posterboard titled . . . Mondays Make Me . . . or . . . BROTHERS AND SISTERS ARE . . . or . . . Things That Bother Me. 3). Cover a work table with brown wrapping paper and just place several pens, pencils, and colored markers in a box near it. This one you might title: IT'S TOUGH BEING A KID BECAUSE . . . 4). Tape a large sheet of white paper on a wall. Place a stack of magazines and newspapers near by, and some scissors and glue. You might title this: GREEN IS . . . or IT MAKES ME SAD. For some additional inspiration students can listen to "Graffiti" a song from one of Good Apples Albums titled . . . **Dandy-Lions Never Roar.**

..... and here are some samples to help you get started .......

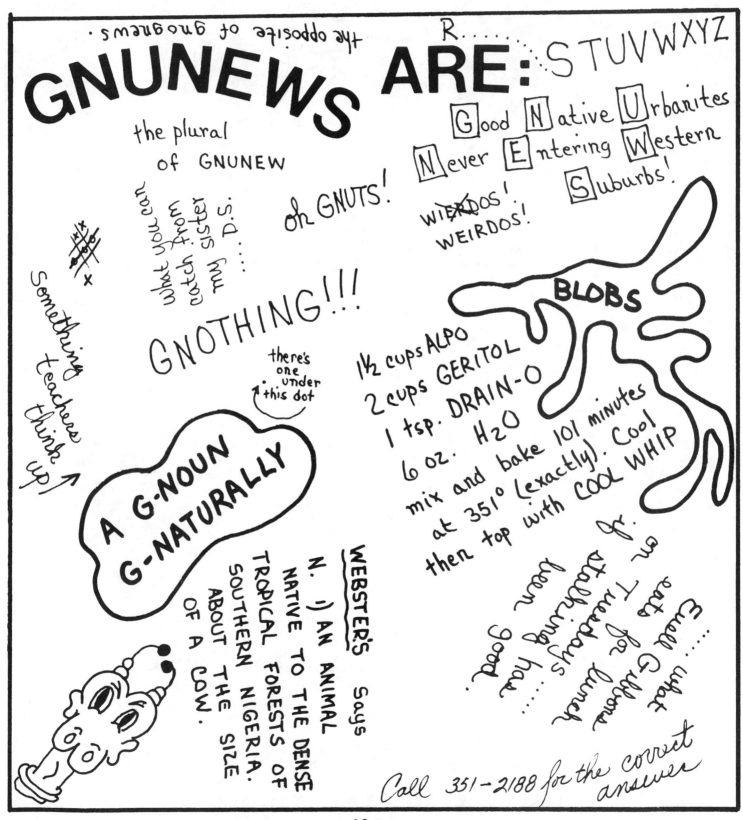

.... graffiti murals are another example illustrating that creative writing does not have to be long .... they are also a great way to allow for brainstorming.

to improve this classroom

we could..... GET RID OF YOU KNOW WHO

Who! I didn't know we had owls in this room

DRAW FLOWERS EVERY-WHERE

just kindly leave the room alone

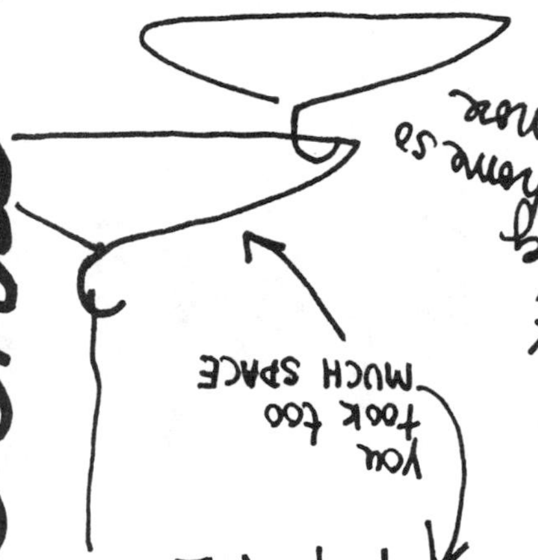

Maybe at least it would look nicer. ¿ not so dead ?

TNT

PLAY: MUSIC
Sign here if you agree
TOM   Sue
Sarah  Barry
BRIAN  Peg

Do more fun stuff like in MATH last FRI.

EVERYBODY SHOULD NOT SHOUT QUITE S OOOOOO MUCH

and this means YOU

NO!

Yes it would

I wouldn't. be fun?

wouldn't decorating that whole day spend

HANG THINGS FROM THE CEILING SO WOULDN'T IT LOOK SO TALL

you took too MUCH SPACE

Hang pictures from home & hang school

This place looked more unexpectedly bring something from home so like a living room.

# CREATING WITH YOUR NAME

Because a child's name is her/his personal property, teach the child to write it correctly, but don't insist that it be written with the same precision and in the same style you insist on for other writing. If a child decides that the i's in the signature should be topped with circles rather than dots, so what? It's the kid's name. Settle for dots over the other i's in his/her writing, but let the child develop a personalized signature. That signature will follow her/him throughout life — such a personal part of a person should not be teacher designed or dictated. It should be the person's own unique invention. Who knows? That signature may one day be a valued part of an expensive oil painting, inscribed on the bottom of silver bowls, or inscribed on U. S. Currency. You never know who a kid may be some day. Treat him/her with respect while he/she is small, and you won't grow up to regret it! Besides, if you don't treat kids with respect, you have some growing up to do.

The name PAUL on the preceding page illustrates an interesting way to feature a child's interests, hobbies, likes and dislikes. Cut the child's name from a sheet of posterboard. The child then covers the name with drawings, cut outs, and actual things he likes, enjoys doing, etc. Display the names of the entire class at once, or spotlight one child at a time. Place all the students' names just outside the classroom, on the hall wall or around the door frame. This will let others know who lives inside. Teacher, be sure to make your name collage, too. You might show your children how important you think they are by pasting a snapshot of each of them on your name collage. Hey! Wouldn't it be cool to cover the whole hall with a name collage from everyone on the entire school?

Summer          Colorado          squi D
                    alabamA           quO te
aU tumn         deL aware         quee N
                    Vermont                A qua
wint Er         indI ana          qui L t
                    oregoN            squa D ron

Children's names are important to them, an intimate part of their lives. So these pages contain a number of creative writing ideas focusing on the child's name. These ideas are from a good friend of Good Apple . . . Dormalee Lindberg, SIU - Carbondale.

M ouse          R ice           lam B
E lephant                       l ia  R
L ion           O ats           l eve E    C harles
I guana                         l ear N    H enry
S alamander     G rains         l an  D    A dam
S nake                          l av  A    D erek
A nteater       E ars of Corn

                R ye

Name lists give children needed practice, using their names as a basis. On a child's birthday, let all students use the child's name. Write the name vertically on the left side of the page. Give the children a category, then let him/her write all the words in that category that begin with or contain the letters in his/her name.

The idea illustrated on the next page uses names to make all-over gift wrap designs. This may be done with a single color, tints, and shades of the same color, or a wild variety of bright colors. Use crayon, felt-tip pens, magic markers, or colored pencils on newsprint, mural paper, newspapers (want-ads are good), or tissue paper. Many variations can be made, using names and/or initials creatively. You can even make a class blanket or quilt by writing names creatively. Have each child create his/her name design on a piece of 8½" x 11" white paper. Collect all efforts. Mount each on a sheet of construction paper and tape together on the reverse side and hang the entire class quilt on a hall wall.

VICKISUELINDBERGVICKISUELINDBERG
VICKISUELINDBERGVICKISUELINDBERG
VICKISUELINDBERGVICKISUELINDBERG
VICKISUELINDBERGVICKISUELINDBERG
VICKISUELINDBERGVICKISUELINDBERG
VICKISUELINDBERGVICKISUELINDBERG
VICKISUELINDBERGVICKISUELINDBERG
VICKISUELINDBERGVICKISUELINDBERG

Most students feel comfortable about their name. It is easy for them to relate to. It is also easy for them to be creative about themselves. It is easy for them to involve themselves in the plots of creative stories. They have a background of information about their lives. Allow your students opportunities to write about what they know best . . . themselves.

Every student is forced to write a haiku sometime during his/her school career. We think it is easy for them because the poetic form of a haiku is not difficult. We must remember the Japanese have been practicing this art for hundred of years and it is threatening to a child to try to create something as good. They can, however, do quite well writing haikus about themselves. The form remains the same but the subject area is more relevant.

Try this idea for a week. Have your students keep a diary for a week while they are at school. Each hour on the hour or as close as the schedule permits have your students write in their diary for five minutes. They can write about what happened the previous hour, how they feel, what they are worrying about, what they are thinking . . . just write. On Friday afternoon collect the diaries. Keep them over the weekend. Promise your students you won't peek. Then on the following Monday return them and allow students to read them again and write about a week at school.

Here is a list of possible creative writing topics focusing on the students' lives and names.

1. Have each student write a story telling how their name actually became a name. You might wish to talk about a couple of names like Hunter and Baker and how those became the family name for many people.

2. Students always enjoy writing an auto-

dormaleedormaleedormaleedormaleedormaleedormalee
maleedormaleedormaleedormaleedormaleedormalee
eedormaleedormaleedormaleedormaleedormaleedor
dormaleedormaleedormaleedormaleedormaleedormalee
maleedormaleedormaleedormaleedormaleedormalee
eedormaleedormaleedormaleedormaleedormaleedormal
dormaleedormaleedormaleedormaleedormaleedormalee
maleedormaleedormaleedormaleedormaleedormaleedor
eedormaleedormaleedormaleedormaleedormaleedormal
dormaleedormaleedormaleedormaleedormaleedormalee
maleedormaleedormaleedormaleedormaleedormaleedor

biography. This can be done in several sessions. Students write one chapter per week. Chapters could be titled, The Day I Was Born, My First Day at School, A History of My First Two Years of Living, My Proudest Moment, and My Future is Up to Me. Allow the students some choice in what they wish to title chapters. No student should be forced to write about a phase of his/her life that he does not wish to share.

Below you see the name Vicki used to make a reflection cutout. The child writes her/his name making it thick enough to be cut out. Then the name is folded over and cut out. This produces the name and its reflection. The cut out names can be used as a border design around a bulletin board or above the chalkboard. Or turn your name into a "Creature Feature." Have students experiment with their name cut-outs and create something from the shapes. Many times the designs become as complex as the personality of the child it belongs to. Extend this activity to include a creative writing activity by the students. The writing activity could be titled . . . MY NAME CREATES.

# create A CINQUAIN about YOURSELF

Ryan
freckled    bespeckled
Smiling - Spinning - Spoofing
like a winning SuperBowl team
PRIDE

A cinquain is a five line poem. There are many variations on the basic form. Have your students write a cinquain about themselves. Perhaps introduce this activity with a cinquain you have written about yourself.

A sample form to follow is:

FIRST LINE      Title / students' name

SECOND LINE   Two adjectives of descriptive words

THIRD LINE      Three verbs

FOURTH LINE   a simile (like a . . or as a . .)

FIFTH LINE      a synonym for the first line.

# TWENTY WORDS

Now that you and your students are into writing phrases and descriptive thoughts, this is a good activity to try.

Have each of your students make a list of 20 words that they like. They can like a word for its sound, its meaning, because they like to say it, or because they just like it. It doesn't matter why.

The results might be similar to the following list.

| | | | |
|---|---|---|---|
| 1. | OPAQUE | 11. | WHIMSICAL |
| 2. | TURQUOISE | 12. | DAWN |
| 3. | LOLLIPOP | 13. | SERENE |
| 4. | SLEEK | 14. | CHOIR |
| 5. | RHYTHMIC | 15. | LOVE |
| 6. | HIGHWAY | 16. | LEISURE |
| 7. | PAISLEY | 17. | ORCHESTRA |
| 8. | GROWING | 18. | LUNCH |
| 9. | FLUID | 19. | WINDING |
| 10. | WHISPERING | 20. | BRISK |

Next allow the students to begin combining the words into pairs and phrases. It should be permissible to change the form and endings of any word. This should be encouraged. Each student should try to come up with several phrases. For example:

a lovely, serene dawn

sleek, winding highways

brisk, winding orchestration

brisk, opaque dawn

fluid orchestra

rhythmic leisure of lunch

serene, leisure love

a whispering, whimsical, winding choir

These phrases do not necessarily need to make sense. Students should try to create phrases that can be visualized. They should experiment by pairing words that don't seem to go together.

Next allow the students to add more and more words to the phrases they have created. Words that will further develop a vision, a feeling, or a mood. The phrases can then grow to be similar to these:

a sleek, opaque, turquoise tinted lollipop

the serenity of a leisurely, lonely lunch

a sleek, fluid highway winding past whispering, paisley fields

whimsical, rhythmic, paisley patterns

a fluid, whispering orchestra and a serene choir

whimsical, winding, paisley patterns called highways cross our nation

the dawn of a brisk, growing love

When small groups of students have finished allow them to exchange ideas and lists and even add to the ideas of fellow classmates. This activity can continue growing and could last several days.

Have your students bring plastic bottles and jugs, cleaned and delabeled, but with lids. These containers will become envelopes. Addresses can be taped on the jugs, or printed directly on with permanent markers. A variety of notes and letters, can be rolled and tied with bright yarn or ribbon and dropped inside. Your students might wish to write seven short notes, roll and tie them, and label them Sunday, Monday, Tuesday, etc. Marbles, gum, wrapped penny candy, and trinkets are just a few of many items that can also be placed inside. Students might also glue a picture on a piece of light cardboard, cut it like a puzzle and drop it into the jug piece by piece. The jugs can then be mailed to a cousin, friend, or grandparent . . . . . or they can be exchanged with another student. You might like to have the students draw names and send a jug to the person whose name they drew.

# WRITE FOR <u>FREE</u> MATERIALS

Remember all the advertisements and all the coupons, you have seen in magazines. Here is your opportunity to try your luck. This is your chance to try to receive something absolutely FREE.

Have each student write a letter requesting free materials for classroom use. Who will benefit? The student and the classroom. Many new learning ideas and materials can be gained. Most any book store carries several paperback books listing sources of free and inexpensive materials. Most professional magazines contain offers from manufacturers.

Several places for students to write to are tourist bureaus, Chambers of Commerce, and government agencies. You can stock your classroom with a lot of valuable information.

MARY BORDERS
126 CHULA VISTA
SAN PEDRO, CA 94351

## "A.... WHAT-IS-MISSING? LETTER"

13¢

Your students will have a lot of fun making a "WHAT-IS-MISSING" letter. It is simple to do, yet it can become very difficult. So the idea is adaptable to all abilities of students. Best of all, every child can have success.

Each student writes a letter to a friend, or to the rest of the class . . . but . . . before he begins he decides what will be missing from his letter.

For Example: all the "a's", or all the "a's" that sound long a, or the second letter of each word, or even every other word. When the letter is completed it can be taped to the chalkboard or wall and everyone can try to discover what is missing.

*a relic from the past.......*

U.S. POSTAL SERVICE, MIAMI, FL JUN 1 '7

CONSERVE OUR WILDLIFE 12

Have students pretend they have just found an old trunk in their attic, basement, or shed. In that old trunk they find a letter that was written over 100 years ago. Who sent the letter? Who received the letter? Was the sentence structure different? Were words used that we no longer use today? What were the topics of conversation? The answers to all of these questions must be made by the students. Perhaps have a class discussion before writing begins. Each student should try to reproduce a letter.

TO MAKE PAPER LOOK OLD: 1) Dip in strong tea solution, 2) Crumple and then press with an iron between two pieces of cloth, 3) Tape paper to floor and walk over it several times, 4) After the paper is written on, wet wash it with ½ starch and ½ water, or with sizing, and 5) Burn the edges and tint with brown food coloring.

# BUT WHO CAN I WRITE TO:

POSTAL SERVICE 15¢ UNITED STATES

1. Use a sports magazine to help you write a fan letter to a sports figure. From the magazine cut as many usable words as you can find and paste them on your letter. You can print any words you need to use and can't find.

2. Write a letter to an animal you would like to have for a pet. The only problem is . . . . this animal has had several offers. You must convince him that you want him, will give him a good home, and feed him well.

3. Pretend you are a historical figure. Write a letter to another famous person who lived during your lifetime.

4. Write a letter describing the type of life you lead from day to day. This letter will be buried in a vault and will be read in 2100.

5. Write a letter to a friend but cut pictures from magazines and paste them on it to take the place of as many words as possible.

6. Make a hieroglyphic letter . . . . . . . similar to the ones of the Ancient Egyptians. Or it can be similar to symbols used by American Indians of 100 years ago.

7. Write a letter to the author of a book you have just read. Tell the author what you liked and disliked about the book.

8. Write a puzzle letter. When you have completed the letter turn it over and draw puzzle shaped pieces. Cut the pieces apart and actually mail it to a friend. In the letter you write be sure to ask the friend to send a similar letter to you in return.

9. Tape a letter on the tape recorder and send it to another classroom.

# ALPHABET SOUP LETTERS

All you need is a few packages of dried alphabet soup and all the students in your class can enjoy this project. You will also need glue for everyone and a piece of dark construction paper for every student. The students simply write their letters by gluing the soup letters on the construction paper. When finished and the glue is dry the letters can be painted with tempera.

# CAN BE LOTS OF FUN

BRYAN BOYER
7216 S. CHARLES ST
So MIAMI, FL 23362

Write a letter to yourself. Ask yourself some questions. Mail the letter. When you receive the letter answer the questions truthfully. You may wish to mail the same letter to someone else. Ask the same questions. Have him/her answer and return the letter. Then you can compare and see if others look at you the same as you look at yourself.

. . . write a fan letter to your favorite singing idol . . . or write a letter to your parents thanking them for some little something they have done for you . . . or write to your Congressman, Senator, or the President of the United States and express your opinion on an important issue of the day . . . or write to the editor of your local newspaper . . . or write to Sally Swashbuckle, she has not received a letter for over 74 years . . . or write to a television station and praise or criticize something you have seen on the station recently . . . or write to the manufacturer of a product you recently purchased and have a complaint about . . . or write to someone you have been meaning to write to for a long time . . . or write to a public servant who has been doing a good job and may need a little thanks . . . and don't forget Santa.

Would you believe a CREATIVE WRITING CENTER that's easy to make? Would you believe that it could last all year long? Would you believe that it will sit right on the corner of your desk, or even in the chalk tray? Do believe it! The ideas on the next few pages will help you get started.

## WHAT YOU WILL NEED TO GET STARTED

One 3" x 5" metal file box full of index cards.
Some dividers that can easily be made from construction paper.
A few photographs or pictures from the newspaper or from magazines.
. . . and that is all . . .

## DIRECTIONS TO THE STUDENTS:

These directions or similar ones to better meet the needs of your students should be typed or printed on two of the 3" x 5" index cards. Then they should be laminated with clear contact paper and placed in the front of the metal file box.

1. You must do each of the activities under "Special Assignments."

2. You must do at least 2 of the activities in each of the additional sections.

3. At least one assignment must be completed each week and handed in on Friday.

4. Completed work should be kept by you in a folder that is available when conferences are held.

5. Each assignment should be dated when it is completed and before it is placed in your folder.

6. All required work (Directions No. 1 and No. 2) must be completed by February 27.

7. Assignments will be graded equally on:
   a. 1/3 of grade creativity
   b. 1/3 of grade grammar
   c. 1/3 of grade neatness, spelling.

## A THOUGHT ABOUT CREATIVITY

Setting limits, goals, etc., does not have to inhibit creativity. It can and many times it does. It will not if you have a climate in your classroom that rewards and encourages creative efforts. Students should be consulted about grades, spelling, and neatness. A grade many times should be a joint effort by student and teacher. Stress the importance of creative thinking in this center. If papers are not neat or if there are numerous spelling errors, perhaps a chance for revision of these errors is in order.

A typical section card could look like the following one. Instead of drawing a picture, you may wish to just make the card colorful or cut a picture from a magazine and glue. You may wish to color code this section card and color code each of the activity cards that are placed behind it.

## POSSIBLE SECTIONS

Special Assignments
Just Suppose Topics
Writing Descriptions
From a Picture
Rewriting
Plots
About Yourself
Writing Letters

You may wish to have many more additional sections. Those listed will be developed further in this book to help you and your students get started.

Possible activity cards students would find behind the Special Assignments section could include:

1. Write a critique of a television program you have recently seen.

2. Write a newspaper article about something that happened in your neighborhood recently.

3. Design a magazine advertisement page for a new product you invented called "FARFELS."

4. Write 2 want ads. One for something you would like to sell and one for something you would like to buy.

A sample activity card might look like this.

5. Invent a new word and develop a dictionary entry for it.

6. Alhoa is a small island in the Pacific Ocean. Write about it as you might expect it to appear in an encyclopedia.

7. Design a book jacket for a library book you have recently read.

8. Write two poems. One poem should rhyme and the other should not.

Possible topics/activities for the **About Yourself** section.

1. There is no one like me. When you read this story you will see.

2. If I could, this is what I would improve about today's world.

3. I always look forward to ................ because ................ .

4. I feel proud when ................ .

5. I am really in favor of ................ because ................ .

6. The hardest problem I have ever faced.

7. Things that make me happy. Make a list.

8. The scariest time of all.

9. I know how it feels to be sad.

10. Keep a diary for one month. You must write in it every day.

11. Write a one-paragraph autobiography.

12. Write a one-paragraph summary of what life has been like for you. One paragraph for each year you have lived. Make this as factual as possible.

13. Predict your future life ................ . Write where you will be and what you will be doing for every five years you expect to live.

14. Make a list of your favorite tastes and smells.

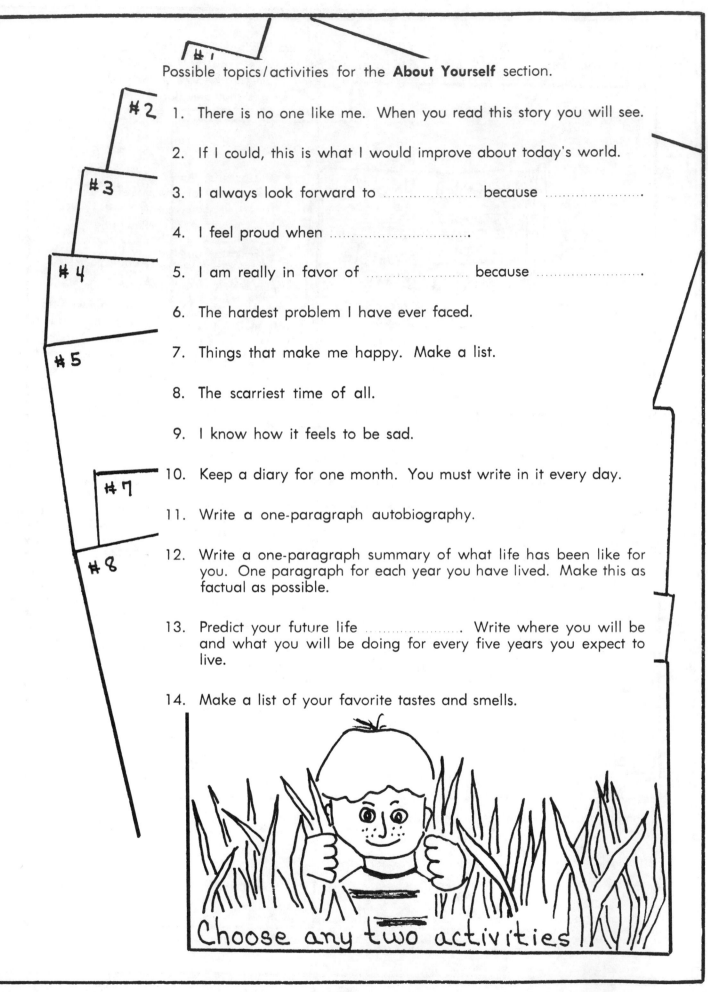

Choose any two activities

# IDEAS for More Sections

## PLOTS

1. the heat of the desert sun, a broken down car, a gold rush.
2. peanut butter, an entire day to do what you want, and Bill Cosby.
3. elephants, petunias, and the back yard fence.
4. heat, fear and irrelevance
5. . . . and the hinge creaked behind me
6. Tarzan, a deserted island, and a shark.
7. . . . closer and closer . . .
8. . . . t h u n d e r, lightning, a n d rain blinded me
9. an Arab Chieftain, a gold ring, and a speeding locomotive
10. 1,000's of ants, one Uncle, and an orchestra playing the William Tell Overture
11. blinding snowstorm, grandma a n d grandpa, a supersonic jet

## TITLES

1. The Somber American
2. In the Heat of the Night
3. The First Thanksgiving on the Moon
4. It's Ridiculous To Put All Your Eggs in One Basket
5. Everything You Needed To Know About Snarkles but Were Afraid To Ask
6. All About Who Flew Who To Kalamazoo
7. Suddenly Showers
8. Shirley Temple's Dimple
9. ?$c%()—
10. Summer Vacation Is My Time of Year
11. The Supersonic Sweathogs
12. The Missing Message from Mandy Murphy
13. Acres Alone
14. Mystical Metallic Monopolies
15. The Egg Experience

## JUST SUPPOSE

1. Pretend to be something that is not alive and write about it . . . a pencil, a wastebasket, a cigar, a key hole . . . it's your choice
2. What do clouds think of people?
3. Write a story incorporating as many name brands as possible . . . the names of soaps, cigarettes, cars, things to drink, etc.
4. My last 3 days before going blind.
5. The night was still, broken only by the shrill screeches of a distant owl. The black, narrow house looked forbidding in the pale moonlight. The leaves which were still on the trees made rustling sounds as a faint breeze blew . . .
6. . . . suddenly I could no longer control the laughter that was . . .
7. A LOPLOP, a most remarkable bird, suddenly flew in the window of your room and began telling you about his adventures.

## DESCRIPTIONS

1. the look of a person who is totally happy.
2. the taste of bananas.
3. the feeling in the pit of your stomach when you are about to be punished.
4. describe what would most a m a z e George Washington, Abraham Lincoln, or Benjamin Franklin if they could visit the United States for a day in the present year.
5. the exact color of a lake.
6. how you feel when your pants are too tight.
7. autumn leaves compared to spring leaves.
8. . . . a skillet . . .
9. the smell of perfume
10. how Miss Muffet felt when she saw the spider.
11. what the spider felt as he approached Miss Muffet

# Rewriting

This section of the Creative Writing Center will require not only a little research by the students, but also will require them to use their imaginations. The threat of being wrong is absent because there is no "one correct answer" to any of the activities. Instead the possible answers are almost limitless. Encourage your students not only to use their creative thinking abilities, but also their values and accumulated knowledge.

1. Rewrite the "Gettysburg Address"

2. Choose any nursery rhyme and rewrite it at least two different ways.

3. Rewrite "Twas the Night Before Christmas" . . . it should be titled "Twas the Day After Christmas".

4. Update some part of your school's policy . . . maybe the sections dealing with dress code, truancy, or gum chewing.

5. Change the ending of your favorite fairy tale so that it is sad rather than happy.

6. Find a short article in the newspaper. Circle all the adjectives. Think of synonyms for the circled adjectives and rewrite the article.

7. Change some of the lyrics to a favorite song . . . maybe you will make it even better.

8. Rewrite the directions for this Learning Center if you think they could be improved.

9. Choose one of your previous efforts from this Learning Center. Rewrite it changing anything you desire. You may turn it in again if you think you could get a better grade because of your additional effort.

10. Redesign your report card. Make it better — report to your parents what you feel is important for them to know about your efforts in school.

# Some More Ideas

1. It was a cold, windy night and you were perched atop one of the two big trees in a cemetery. What did you see? What did you hear? What happened?

2. You woke up one morning and found that there was nobody in your house or city; actually there was no one in the whole world but you. What did you do? What were your thoughts and feelings?

3. Write the biography of a seed.

4. Write about ottatas and their world.

5. What is time?

6. Why rabbits never wear earmuffs.

7. Wild things and magic rings.

8. The day a crocodile swam out of the faucet and made jell-o in the bathtub.

9. Congratulations! You have just inherited 2,200,202 fish.

10. What would happen to a person who ate a clock for breakfast?

11. The day the crab monsters attacked.

12. Biographical data on the first space creature that was captured on Earth.

13. Write your will and your epitaph.

You may wish to include a picture section in your Creative Writing Learning Center. Use postcards, photographs, and pictures from magazines. Just mount each on a 3" x 5" index card. These pictures should serve as motivation for creative writing. Directions for this section might be similar to the following:

Use one of the pictures as motivation for a creative story or paragraph. To start, make a list of everything you see and feel while looking at the picture. Then incorporate those ideas you listed into your writing effort.

Another group of pictures could be used so students could simply write titles or captions for them. Each student could choose the picture which most intrigued him and on the back side write several possible titles.

## SOME ADDITIONAL TIPS TO CONSIDER

It might be wise to have a box (cover it with bright patterned contact paper) to hold manila folders containing each student's efforts. One folder per student filed in alphabetical order. In this could also be placed the progress chart (sample next page).

Be sure to place several blank cards in each section of your Creative Writing Box. On these blank cards your students can contribute ideas appropriate for that section.

It is best to cover both sides of all the index cards with clear contact paper.

Be sure to number each activity card in each section. This makes for more accurate record keeping.

# Student Progress Chart

.............................................................................................. Name

| Required Assignments | Date Completed | Student/Teacher Conference Results |
|---|---|---|
| No. 1 | | |
| No. 2 | | |
| No. 3 | | |
| No. 4 | | |
| No. 5 | | |
| No. 6 | | |

| Activity Sections | Card No. | Date Completed | Student/Teacher Conference Results |
|---|---|---|---|
| Titles | | | |
| Plots | | | |
| About Yourself | | | |
| Rewriting | | | |
| Descriptions | | | |
| From A Picture | | | |
| Just Suppose | | | |

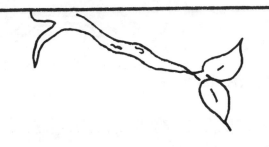

# CREATIVE WRITING WITH RELEVANCE

## CREATIVE WRITING WITH RELEVANCE

This section of the Good Apple Creative Writing Book contains 17 ready-to-use creative writing activity sheets. All you will need to do is duplicate the actual pages.

As you will see, each activity sheet is designed to accomplish several goals. First, on each sheet are several questions to motivate the students' creative thinking concerning the topic. These questions and things to think about are included to encourage the student to think, brainstorm, be fluent of thought, and be flexible of thought before he actually begins to write. These questions ask the student to generate many ideas/thoughts and then evaluate those thoughts into a written effort. Second, the questions/thoughts are designed to provide focus for class discussions. Many times, having the class discuss a topic before attempting to write about it, will allow many students to produce a more creative result.

Most of all, these creative writing activities combine creative thinking or skill building. Writing letters (business and friendly), thank you notes, invitations, announcements, drawing maps, etc., are all practical writing experiences. As adults, your students will need to be able to do this type of writing. It is relevant.

It is nice to be able to write a critique, a book report, and an essay. But seldom, past the classroom environment, does the average person ever have to do this again. Most of the activities in this section will give the student an opportunity to learn through experience, with writing they will use in their everyday adult life.

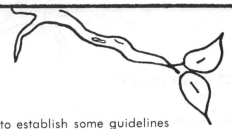

Before beginning this unit, you will probably wish to establish some guidelines for your students.

1. Should every student attempt all of these activities?
2. How many and which activities should be required?
3. What are the grading criteria? The student has a right to know this before he begins.
4. How long should this unit of activities last?
5. Should most of the work be done independently?
6. Should the students work on the same activity at the same time?
7. How can I best introduce these activities and how can I provide additional motivation?
8. Which activities will I need to redesign to better fit the age and abilities of my students?

You and your students will need to accumulate samples of the following before beginning the unit.

1. Newspaper/magazine advertisements.
2. Business letters and a beginning typing book.
3. Newspapers and magazine interviews.
4. A variety of greeting cards.
5. Editorials from newspapers/magazines.
6. Thank-you notes.
7. Letters to the editor/publisher.
8. A copy of **Sport** and **Sports Illustrated** and **Women's Sport** magazines. Also several sport items from the newspaper.
9. Samples of invitations to parties, graduations, weddings, and anniversaries.
10. 5 newspaper headlines. 5 newspaper stories with the headlines clipped off.
11. A variety of travel brochures.
12. 6 cartoons from newspapers/magazines. A Sunday funnies supplement from newspaper
13. Fashion articles and pictures from newspapers/magazines. A copy of **Vogue** or **Harpers Bazaar.**

# ADVERTISEMENT POSTER

1. THINK! Find a place where you can think.

   THINK about advertisements — those you have seen in magazines and news-papers — those you have seen on television. What about those you have seen while riding in a car?

   THINK of all the advertisements that have appealed to you.

   THINK of those that were clever.

   THINK of those that made you want to buy the product.

2. Look at some of the advertisements in the Advertisement Folder. Why do they appeal or not appeal to you? What is the purpose of any advertisement?

   ...................................................................................................................

   ...................................................................................................................

   ...................................................................................................................

3. Think about a product that you might like to sell. On a sheet of paper draw a sketch of that product.

   a. It could be a product you already know about.

   b. It could be a product you invent or have invented and would like to try to sell.

   c. Mess around with your drawing — keep trying to make it more attractive . . . more appealing.

   d. Be sure you have a good drawing and a really good slogan.

   e. Have you listed the price? Do you need to? Have you explained the uses? Have you told where the product can be purchased?

4. On a sheet of poster paper or large sheet of manila paper make a final copy of your advertisement. Pretend that your final copy will appear in a newspaper, magazine, or on a billboard. GOOD LUCK!

5. When you are finished hang your poster on the classroom wall.

# BUSINESS LETTERS

1. What is a business letter?

   .............................................................................
   .............................................................................
   .............................................................................
   .............................................................................
   .............................................................................
   .............................................................................

2. How is a business letter different from a friendly letter?

   .............................................................................
   .............................................................................
   .............................................................................
   .............................................................................
   .............................................................................
   .............................................................................

3. Could a letter be a combination of a business letter and a friendly letter? How? Why?

   .............................................................................
   .............................................................................
   .............................................................................
   .............................................................................
   .............................................................................

4. List all the types of, or reasons for business letters you can think of. If you were a business man, why would you or your secretary write business letters?

5. Study the sample business letters in the English and typing books. Some real samples can be found in the manila folder box.

6. Write a business letter. Staple it to the back of this sheet.

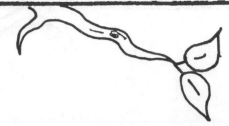

# NEWSPAPER OR MAGAZINE INTERVIEW

1. Find some interviews in the school newspaper, local newspaper or in a magazine. Some can also be found in the interview folder.

   a. Read a couple of interviews that you find. Think about how the conversation between the two people was reported.

2. Think of someone interesting to interview. It could be:

   a. a famous person (living or dead).

   b. the principal of your school.

   c. someone in your community who has an interesting hobby or job.

   d. someone in your community who has traveled to an interesting place.

   e. your parent or grandparent.

   f. a classmate.

3. Pretend you are conducting an interview. You ask the questions and also supply the answers the way you think the person you are interviewing would answer them.

   a. Use a question and answer style of writing.

4. Now conduct an actual interview. Make a set of questions for a specific person you are going to interview. Record his responses. Write the interview.

   a. Write this interview in story form. Do not use a question/answer form.

5. Staple both interviews to this paper.

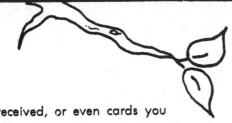

## GREETING CARDS

1. Think of the greeting cards you have sent or received, or even cards you have just seen in stores.

    a. What were they like? What did they say? Did you like them? What were they shaped like? How did they fold?

    b. Study the samples in the Greeting Card Folder.

2. Make three greeting cards. Each should be a different type for a different occasion. Place the completed cards in your finished work folder.

3. Think again about all of the greeting cards you have sent or received. Make a list of all the reasons or occasions a person might send or receive a greeting card.

    .......................................   .......................................   .......................................
    .......................................   .......................................   .......................................
    .......................................   .......................................   .......................................
    .......................................   .......................................   .......................................
    .......................................   .......................................   .......................................
    .......................................   .......................................   .......................................
    .......................................   .......................................   .......................................
    .......................................   .......................................   .......................................

4. Study your list and try to group the reasons and occasions into categories. For example a category might be holidays. Decide on several categories and place each type you listed in one of the categories.

5. What do you feel is the most common type of greeting card sent? Why?

    ...........................................................................................................
    ...........................................................................................................
    ...........................................................................................................

## NEWSPAPER EDITORIAL***

1. Do some research on the word editorial. What is its meaning?

   a. How is an editorial different from a regular newspaper story?

   b. How is an editorial different from a letter to the editor?

   c. Editor and edition are similar words. What do they mean?

   d. Can you find some other words that come from the same root word?

2. What is the job of a newspaper editor? Explain briefly.

   .................................................................................................................

   .................................................................................................................

   .................................................................................................................

   .................................................................................................................

   .................................................................................................................

   .................................................................................................................

   .................................................................................................................

   .................................................................................................................

   .................................................................................................................

3. Pretend you are a newspaper editor. Write an editorial for your paper.

   a. Choose a topic that is of interest and importance to to you.

   b. Write it on a separate page and attach it to this work sheet.

*** See NEWSPAPER EDITORIAL FOLDER for some sample editorials.

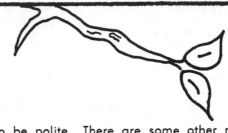

## THANK YOU NOTES

1. A person should send a thank-you note just to be polite. There are some other reasons. Can you think of some?

   .................................................................................................................
   .................................................................................................................
   .................................................................................................................
   .................................................................................................................

2. Pretend you are going to give a lesson on thank-you notes. Make a set of guidelines for people to follow in order for them to write a thank-you note.

   .................................................................................................................
   .................................................................................................................
   .................................................................................................................
   .................................................................................................................
   .................................................................................................................

3. Write a thank-you note for any **three** of the following:

   a. a birthday present from Aunt Maude

   b. a 3-day visit with a friend

   c. a Christmas present you already have

   d. a gift you received when you were sick

   e. to a person who is moving who helped you in scouts while they lived in your community

   f. a friend who helped you give a party

4. You can find some samples in the Thank-You Note Folder.

## A TRAVEL BROCHURE

1. Spend some time looking through the many travel brochures in the Travel Folder.

   a. Notice the pictures, drawings, color, explanations, and maps.

   b. What does the designer show and tell about the place he is describing?

   c. How does the designer make a place look inviting?

   d. What important information is included?

2. Think of some places you would like to visit. It could be a city, state, country, building, park, or scenic spot.

3. Choose your favorite place and design a travel brochure about it.

4. You will need factual knowledge so use resource materials in the library.

5. Plan and work carefully. This project should take quite a while to complete. That is OK. Just do a good job.

   a. Be sure to include pictures, drawings, and maps.

   b. Summarize the information you need to include.

   c. Make your brochure neat, colorful and attractive.

6. You may wish to write and get some free information about various cities, states, countries and resorts. If so I will try to give you some addresses.

# SPORTS REPORTING

1. Make a list of as many sporting events as you can think of.

....................................     ....................................     ....................................

....................................     ....................................     ....................................

....................................     ....................................     ....................................

....................................     ....................................     ....................................

....................................     ....................................     ....................................

    a. Decide on some basic categories of sporting events and place each event you listed into one of the categories you have chosen.

2. Look at and read some of the sport stories in the folder including the copies of **Sports** and **Sports Illustrated.**

    a. Study the various ways the sporting events were reported and written.

3. Take a look at the sports headlines in the same folder. Choose any two and write an article to go with the headline.

4. Write a sports story about any one of the following:

    a. the Super Bowl.

    b. the Olympics.

    c. the day I was a sports hero.

    d. the hard life of being an athlete.

    e. what it means to be a good sport.

    f. the World Series.

    g. a really neat sport that few people know about or participate in.

    h. why amateur athletics are better than professional athletics.

    i. when an athlete grows old.

5. Attach your work to this sheet.

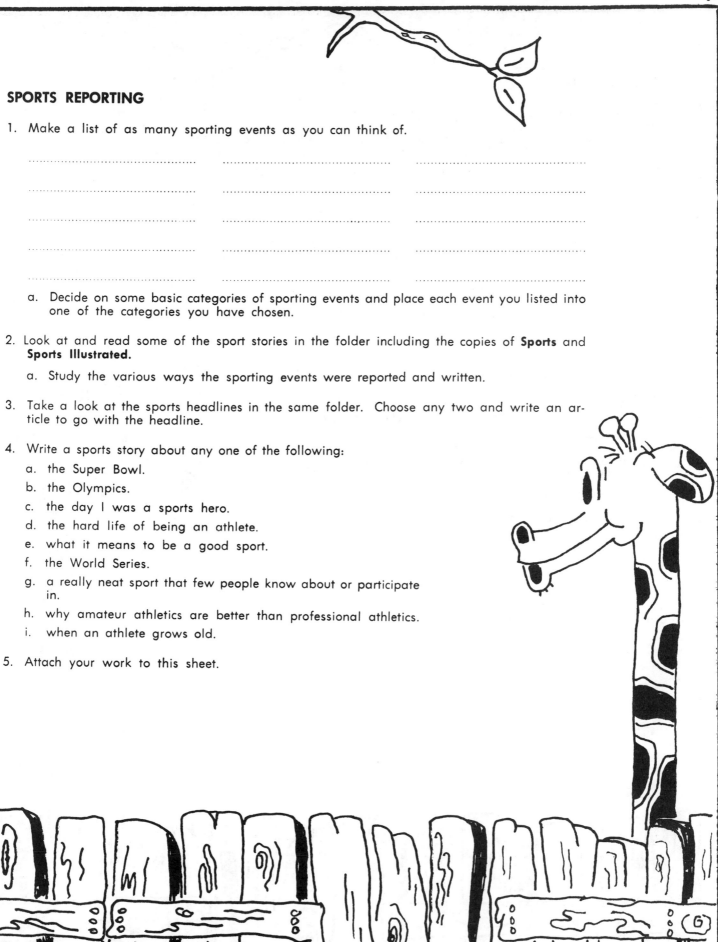

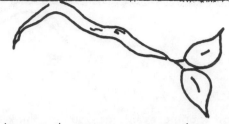

## INVITATIONS

1. Think about invitations to parties and events, that you have sent or received.
   a. What information could you find on the invitation? What did you need to know?

   ...........................................................................................................................................
   ...........................................................................................................................................
   ...........................................................................................................................................
   ...........................................................................................................................................
   ...........................................................................................................................................
   ...........................................................................................................................................
   ...........................................................................................................................................

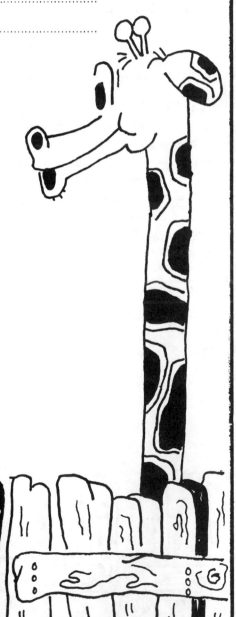

2. Pretend you are having a party. You must send invitations. Design and write an invitation to three of the following occasions:

   a. your birthday party.

   b. a Mother's Day party your school class is giving at school.

   c. a surprise birthday party you are giving for a friend.

   d. a slumber party.

   e. the school athletic banquet.

   f. a Boy/Girl Scout cookout.

3. Some invitations require an R.S.V.P. Write one.

4. Attach your work to this sheet.

5. What does R.S.V.P. mean?

## YOUR AUTOBIOGRAPHY

1. You are to write the true story of your life.

   There are several ways you can do this.

       a. you might present your life in diary form.

       b. a scrapbook with pictures and short explanations would be acceptable.

       c. outline form which included the highlights.

       d. a book approach with chapters for the various years.

2. How is an autobiography different from a biography? .............

   ......................................................................................................

   ......................................................................................................

   ......................................................................................................

3. Make two lists of words. First, list some words with the prefix "bi". Second, list words with the prefix "auto".

   ..................................................    ..................................................

   ..................................................    ..................................................

   ..................................................    ..................................................

   ..................................................    ..................................................

   ..................................................    ..................................................

   ..................................................    ..................................................

4. If you were to try and find the exact truth about someone famous, let's say Joe Namath, which do you feel would be the most factual, his biography or his autobiography? Why? What would be wrong with each? What would be most acceptable about each?

5. Attach your work to this sheet.

## NEWSPAPER HEADLINES

1. Look at the five news headlines in the Headlines Folder. Write a one-sentence statement telling what you think the story was about.

   1. ......................................................................................................
   2. ......................................................................................................
   3. ......................................................................................................
   4. ......................................................................................................
   5. ......................................................................................................

2. Write news headlines for any five stories in your reading book.

   1. ......................................................................................................
   2. ......................................................................................................
   3. ......................................................................................................
   4. ......................................................................................................
   5. ......................................................................................................

3. Read any five of the news articles found in the headlines folder and write news headlines for them.

   1. ......................................................................................................
   2. ......................................................................................................
   3. ......................................................................................................
   4. ......................................................................................................
   5. ......................................................................................................

4. Write a headline for each of the following:
   a. the story of Little Red Ridinghood.
   b. the death of a very famous person.
   c. our classroom elections.
   d. astronauts having trouble during their space flight.
   e. the school team.
   f. the end of a war.

5. Write a short newspaper story for any three of the following headlines:
   a. THE PRESIDENT RETURNS
   b. AIR CRASH KILLS & INJURES 72
   c. DONNIE OSMOND WINS AWARD
   d. BOMB THREAT — NO HOAX
   e. SELLOUT — TONIGHT — AT STADIUM

6. Attach all work to this sheet.

## LETTER TO THE EDITOR

1. Study some sample letters to the editor from various newspapers and magazines. Some can be found in the Letters-to-the-Editor Folder.

2. Pick a topic that is interesting and important to you and write a letter to the editor stating your opinion.

3. Almost all magazines print letters from the readers.

   a. Study some from the Letters-to-the-Editor Folder and think about whether they agree or disagree with what they read in the magazine.

   b. How are these letters to the editor different from friendly letters?

   c. What guidelines would you suggest to a person who is going to write a letter to a newspaper or magazine?

4. Read an article in any magazine that appeals to you. There are plenty of magazines in the school library. **Time** is a good magazine for this project but choose any you like.

   a. Write a reply to the magazine about the article you choose to read.

   b. It does not have to be a criticism. The reply can just state your thoughts.

   c. You can agree or disagree with the article you read.

   d. You may want to write two. One where you agree and one where you disagree.

## COMIC STRIPS

1. Pick your favorite cartoon or comic strip character and draw the character in the following ways:

   a. a close up of his head and shoulders.

   b. a full view from head to toe.

   c. in a series of actions (3 or 4).

2. Look at the set of cartoons in the Comic-Strip Folder. Write captions for each cartoon. They are numbered 1 to 6.

   a. ..................................................................................

   b. ..................................................................................

   c. ..................................................................................

   d. ..................................................................................

   e. ..................................................................................

   f. ..................................................................................

3. Invent a new comic character. Draw a portrait of this character and an 8-frame comic strip. Be sure to include captions.

4. Can you define these cartoon-associated words?

   a. **action shot** ..............................................................

   b. **cartoon** ..................................................................

   c. **frame** ....................................................................

   d. **caption** ..................................................................

   e. **portrait** ..................................................................

   f. **comic strip** ..............................................................

5. What are the purposes of cartoon and comic strips? Is there more to them than just entertainment?

   ..................................................................................

   ..................................................................................

   ..................................................................................

## SYMBOL DICTIONARY

1. Think of and make a list of, as many symbols as you can. For example: #, X, (, ), +, =

   ............   ............   ............   ............   ............   ............   ............
   ............   ............   ............   ............   ............   ............   ............
   ............   ............   ............   ............   ............   ............   ............
   ............   ............   ............   ............   ............   ............   ............
   ............   ............   ............   ............   ............   ............   ............
   ............   ............   ............   ............   ............   ............   ............
   ............   ............   ............   ............   ............   ............   ............

   and you will think of many more.

2. Make a dictionary of the symbols that you think of. There may be a better way to organize it than alphabetical order. If you think of a better way, use it. Try something different.

3. Go on a symbol search. Look everywhere for symbols. Run up to someone, anyone, and ask him/her for as many symbols as he/she knows. Look in all types of books and magazines.

4. Your dictionary should be as full as you can make it.

5. Is there a difference between symbols and abbreviations? How are they similar? How are they different?

   ....................................................................
   ....................................................................
   ....................................................................
   ....................................................................
   ....................................................................
   ....................................................................

6. Make your dictionary on white writing paper. Fold it in half and your dictionary will be a good size. Or if you wish, buy some small type of notebook. Have fun.

# FASHION DESIGNS AND ARTICLES

1. Look at the fashion articles and collection of fashion pictures in the Fashion Folder. As you look:

   a. think about how the articles and descriptions are written.

   b. think about whether or not you like the various designs.

2. Browse through magazines, newspapers, and catalogs and clip out several fashions that you like.

   a. Carefully mount each fashion on a piece of construction paper.

   b. Write a description of each fashion and glue it on the mounted picture page.

3. Sketch some creations of your own and write descriptions of each article.

4. You may decide to present a fashion show to the class.

   a. The show can be oral with you describing each outfit while it is being shown on the opaque projector.

   b. The show can be a bulletin board display with pictures and written comments.

5. Write a fashion article . . . describe a real or imaginary wedding you recently attended in your fashion article.

## MAPS

1. Draw a map that your teacher could use to find your home. Make the starting point the school building.

2. What must be included on a map in order for it to be good?

.......................................................................................

.......................................................................................

.......................................................................................

.......................................................................................

.......................................................................................

3. Find some maps in a variety of books. Study how these maps communicate with you. How do they help you to understand what they say?

4. Revise the map you made on how to get to your house, if you feel you could do a better job, now that you have studied some maps.

5. Now write a set of directions telling how to get to your house. This should not be a map. It is as if someone asked you how to get to your house, and you told them. Write down what you would say.

6. Compare your map with your written directions. Which is easier to follow? Which was easier to do? Is it easy to write what you would say?

.......................................................................................

.......................................................................................

.......................................................................................

7. Now make one of these maps —

   a. a map of the school room.

   b. a map of your neighborhood.

   c. how to get to the park from your house.

   d. a map of your house.

## A DING-A-LING LETTER

A ding-a-ling letter is a letter written to —

      a.  a movie star you are in love with.

      b.  Ann Landers.

      c.  a TV mail bag show.

      d.  a radio disc jockey.

The author of a ding-a-ling letter hopes the letter will be printed or read by 1,000's of people.  It also is hoped that there will be a reply.

A ding-a-ling letter is —

      a.  stupid.

      b.  meant to be humorous.

      c.  usually a gripe, or complaint or confession.

      d.  sometimes an invitation.

WRITE ONE!    HAVE FUN!    BE HUMOROUS!    GOOD LUCK!    BE CREATIVE!

ONE or 2

CREATIVE WRITING IDEAS

You have just landed in spaceship EARTH on a strange planet. Describe what you see when you open the spaceship door. A different form of life inhabits this planet. What does it look like? How does it communicate?

Write a few sentences in this new language. Name this unknown planet. Describe earth to an inhabitant of this planet. Write a story of a person from this planet playing on your ball team.

# Do Sonny & Cher Share or

What if the sun stopped shining?......The unknown secret of the lost _____.....Disaster strikes!!...... Try to hide a secret message in a type-written page ..... How would it feel to be a doorknob, a rug, a chicken feather, or a spandangle?..... Write an "I WAS THERE" news story. Choose an animal that is most like you and write and tell why.

VIEWPOINT: Many times students are more worried about "the grade" than the creation. You might try this . . . after students have tried, discussed and accumulated several creative writing assignments take a "time out" day so they can look over their accumulated material. Then they can choose one that they think is pretty good. All they have to do before handing it in is dress it up . . . neatness/spelling, etc.

Don't allow grades to kill creative thinking in your classroom. It is easier to get correct spelling than it is to get **GOOD** ideas from many students.

# Don't Use These Ideas......
## Let Them Motivate,
## Better Ones!

Use music and write about the mood it puts you in.. .... Make a group poem/Everybody writes one line.......... Design a dictionary for the future and words to go in it.

Write a paragraph about the most outstanding person you know......

TITLE: How To Ride an Elephant Through a Thorn Forest

Design a dictionary especially for farmers, or nurses, or plumbers, or jockeys, or city people visiting the country........... List all the synonyms/antonyms groovy people have as a part of their vocabularies. .... Write a Who's Who in your Community.

VIEWPOINT: Don't let spelling hangups keep your students from being creative writers. The natural instinct is not to use a word that you are not sure you can spell. It is up to the teacher to eliminate this fear. Allow students to write with dictionaries open. If a word is missed don't count it wrong unless they fail to correct it when you return the paper. Give students a day to correct any misspelled word.

How is a bee hive like Chicago? ..... How is the Queen Bee like the Queen of England? .....

Write a short story about Queenie the Queen Bee who wanted to fly around the world. Pretend you are a bee — your job is to guard the entrance to the hive. Write a story about this. TITLE: One day all the flowers died.

VIEWPOINT: It is the teacher's responsibility to help students feel a need to put their personal thoughts and ideas into written words. It is not always the teacher's responsibility to tell the students what to write about. What to write about is many times best determined by the student.

# Mud pies! A Threatening Sky Two-ton flys! Mysterious Spies and An Onion That Cries

plus other goodies to write about!

Write a diary about your first week on Mars...... Invent a story that explains how/why a famous quotation became famous........ .....Develop a plot for a typical soap opera, titled: THE WAY THE EGG BREAKS ...... Write a story for kindergarten children and illustrate it...... TITLE: How the i got its dot. ..... Become your favorite plant, How do you feel? What is your life like?

VIEWPOINT: It is a lot easier to tame a wild creative idea than it is to build up an idea that lacks luster, imagination and zip. Encourage the creative aspect of your students' writing. Motivate them to diverge and expand. After the idea has been hatched comes the time for refining and improving.

If you were to become an animal what animal would you choose to be? Why? Describe how you would feel.... what would you think about? Describe a heroic deed you once performed. Pretend you become a famous animal entertainer. Describe your act. What problems would you encounter as a wealthy animal. How would you help other animals?

DOFI

VIEWPOINT: Be very careful when evaluating or passing judgment on a student's creative effort. The best approach may be to display all efforts whenever possible and allow students to make their own evaluations. Students will begin to recognize the response that is different (original). They will be able to compare their ability to generate responses (fluency). They may learn that even though they may not be the most fluent, their strength is their ability to take someone else's ideas and elaborate to make it a better idea. Through watching how peers respond they can gain vicariously from their experience and become more flexible.

# More Titles, Thoughts, Ideas, and Such

Explain how the bark on a tree is like a fur coat....... How do giraffes neck and other pets pet?....... Try some code writing...... Make a word montage — cut out from magazines and glue....... Draw a hieroglyphic story ...... Try writing poems for the WORSE VERSE BOOK........ Write a poem about yourself — title it THE GOOD SIDE OF ME .... TITLE: Mother McCredy's Home Remedies ...... Write a poem — LEAFY GREEN WAS NERVOUS ..... Write what you would like your tombstone to say.

VIEWPOINT: Being creative is threatening to students. In general, schools don't encourage originality, flexibility, fluency, and elaboration. Conformity is generally encouraged and rewarded in most schools. It will take a long time for students to feel safe. And they must feel safe to risk being creative. Don't be discouraged. If your first efforts at encouraging creativity fail, don't give up . . . it may take awhile.

# Write a Conversation Between Two Birds or if a toucan you can....

**VIEWPOINT:**

Many times we ask students to come up with a good or clever idea without really providing them time to do so. Even worse we don't provide the training needed to generate ideas. Before students write about anything they need ideas . . . lots of ideas . . . and even more ideas. They need their ideas and the ideas of many others to build with. Allow time for just generating ideas. This can be done individually, in small groups or with the entire class. It is not a waste of time to spend several class periods just generating ideas. If you create a climate that accepts all ideas as they emerge, you and your students will generate tons of ideas. Criticizing and making fun of students' ideas will only squelch the creative flow. When the purpose is generating ideas there is no need for quality . . . the emphasis should be on quantity.

My latest invention will blow your mind .... Make a list of all the synonyms for the word said and then write a conversation........ List all the words you can think of that rhyme with "meow", then write a poem about cats........ What are all the words that begin with Z?     Write about the Best is Last .....  What do you get when you fall in love? ....... TITLE: Zongers are.. ........ Sorry, I've only got 24¢ to my name... .... where does a fly fly — high? ........ write and make something perfectly clear.........

# Getting to know POPCORN

POPCORN

1. Give each student a grain of popcorn. Ask them to write down all the words that describe it (maybe a class list on the board) — have students really examine it — then collect the corn and see if anyone can reclaim his/her exact piece.

2. Now pop some corn — while it is popping have the kids, listen, smell and write down all the words they smell, hear, and feel.

3. Then give each student one popped grain. Have them look closely and write down what they see, touch(feel) and smell. Collect the popped grains, and see if they can identify his/hers.

4. Give each student some to eat while they write THE KERNEL TURNS WHITE

**VIEWPOINT:**

To really learn, students must get involved. They must experience. They must manipulate . . . physically as well as mentally.

Rewrite some of your favorite quotations. "Ask not what your country can do for you, but what you can do for your country"

"I regret I have but one life to _____".

Here are some quotations of Benjamin Franklin. Can you add new endings

"Early to bed & early to rise makes a man _____."

"A penny saved is a _____."

"A stitch in time saves _____ _____."

Design some new quotations. Maybe they will be very famous 25 years from now.

VIEWPOINT: For creative thinking to be a worthwhile experience the teacher must be sold that it is important for students to be able to do this. If you question the usefulness and importance of creative writing and thinking, perhaps it would be better for someone else to introduce activities and motivate your students.

# A RESTAURANT ALL MY OWN

PIZZA PARADISE

A CREATIVE WRITING CONTRACT THAT INCORPORATES A VARIETY OF WRITING ACTIVITIES WITH SKILLS FROM OTHER SUBJECT AREAS.

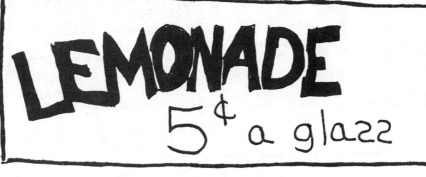

### NOTE TO TEACHER

Your students will enjoy creating their own restaurant. Many will want to do all the suggested activities. The activities shown are only a few of many possible activities. We hope they will serve as examples of what creative thinking/writing activities can be involved in a contract.

Introduce each possible activity carefully and thoroughly. Be sure materials needed to do the activities are readily available to the students. You may wish to hold several class discussions about eating in restaurants before you introduce the activities. Encourage your students to relate their restaurant experiences with fellow class members.

Much of the work on many of the activities can be done by students in their spare time It might be wise to have half hour time segments set aside each day as designated work time.

Stress quality not quantity.

It would be great to take a field trip as part of the introductory activities to this unit. You might plan to visit several types of restaurants in your community. It also might be profitable to invite a restaurant owner and a chef or waiter to your classroom. They could talk about their jobs and answer questions.

This contract is a legal, written agreement between _____, owner of the _____ restaurant, and _____, PRESIDENT, FIRST BANK AND TRUST COMPANY. This contract states your intended efforts to make your restaurant a success. Read carefully all the possible activities. Think carefully — then check ☑ those you decide to accept. All restaurant owners must choose * activities

- ☐ * Activity No. 1
- ☐ * Activity No. 2
- ☐ * Activity No. 3
- ☐ * Activity No. 4
- ☐ * Activity No. 5
- ☐ * Activity No. 6
- ☐ Activity No. 7 — Menu
- ☐ Activity No. 8 — Portrait
- ☐ Activity No. 9 — Story
- ☐ Activity No. 10 — Special of House
- ☐ Activity No. 11 — Blueprint
- ☐ Activity No. 12 — Advertisement

STUDENT - RESTAURANT OWNER

TEACHER - BANK PRESIDENT

DATE

Make a <u>decision</u>   What kind of a restaurant would you like to own?

___ hot dog stand          ___ pizza parlor

___ drive-in               ___ ice cream

___ taco                   ___ very, very fancy

___ smörgäsbord            ___ <u>cafeteria</u>

___ other _____

Now think of ten possible names for your restaurant.

1. _____     6. _____

2. _____     7. _____

3. _____     8. _____

4. _____     9. _____

5. _____     10 _____

Now write the best title you thought of below.

# ACTIVITY #2

Listed below are some jobs that will need to be filled before my restaurant opens __

1. _____  6. _____

2. _____  7. _____

3. _____  8. _____

4. _____  9. _____

5. _____  10. _____

I believe I will need to <u>hire</u> ____ people. The <u>qualifications</u> I will be looking for in the <u>personnel</u> I hire are __

1. _____

2. _____

3. _____

4. _____

5. _____

I have designed an <u>application</u> blank for <u>prospective</u> <u>employees</u> to complete. It is stapled to the back of this page.

**\* ACTIVITY #3**

Below are several ways I thought about designing, writing, printing the name of my restaurant.

Below is the <u>official</u> name

## Price List

## Pizza Paradise

|  | SMALL | LARGE |
|---|---|---|
| Cheese | $3.00 | $3.50 |
| Hamburger | $3.50 | $4.00 |
| Sausage | $3.50 | $4.00 |
| Mushroom | $3.75 | $4.25 |

Add 50¢ for each extra item — onions pepper - olives - bacon

Salads  small 50¢  large $1.00

Coffee 20¢
Tea (Hot or Iced) 25¢
Pepsi
Coke }  20¢ or 30¢
7-Up }

# Guest Check

| TABLE NO. | NO. PEOPLE | 0003652 |
|---|---|---|
|  |  |  |
|  |  |  |
|  |  |  |
|  |  |  |
|  |  |  |
|  |  |  |
|  |  |  |
|  |  |  |
|  |  |  |
|  |  |  |
|  | TAX |  |
|  | TOTAL |  |

THANK YOU FOR COMING

Use the menu to the left and the guest check above and "write up" an order for you and two friends.

Design a guest check for your restaurant and make 2 sample bills. Glue on the back of this page.

ACTIVITY #5

My spelling and vocabulary list of any
10 words underlined in this contract plus
10 more words I use in my restaurant __

1. _____   11. _____

2. _____   12. _____

3. _____   13. _____

4. _____   14. _____

5. _____   15. _____

6. _____   16. _____

7. _____   17. _____

8. _____   18. _____

9. _____   19. _____

10. _____   20. _____

I know the meaning of each word. I
can spell it and I can use it in
a sentence.

Some good things about owning your very own restaurant are:

1.

2.

3.

4.

5.

Some bad, things about owning your very own restaurant are:

1.

2.

3.

4.

If business gets bad, here are some things I will try to do to improve it:

1.

2.

3.

# MENU

Here is the <u>menu</u> for my business <u>establishment</u>

FRONT

BACK

INSIDE

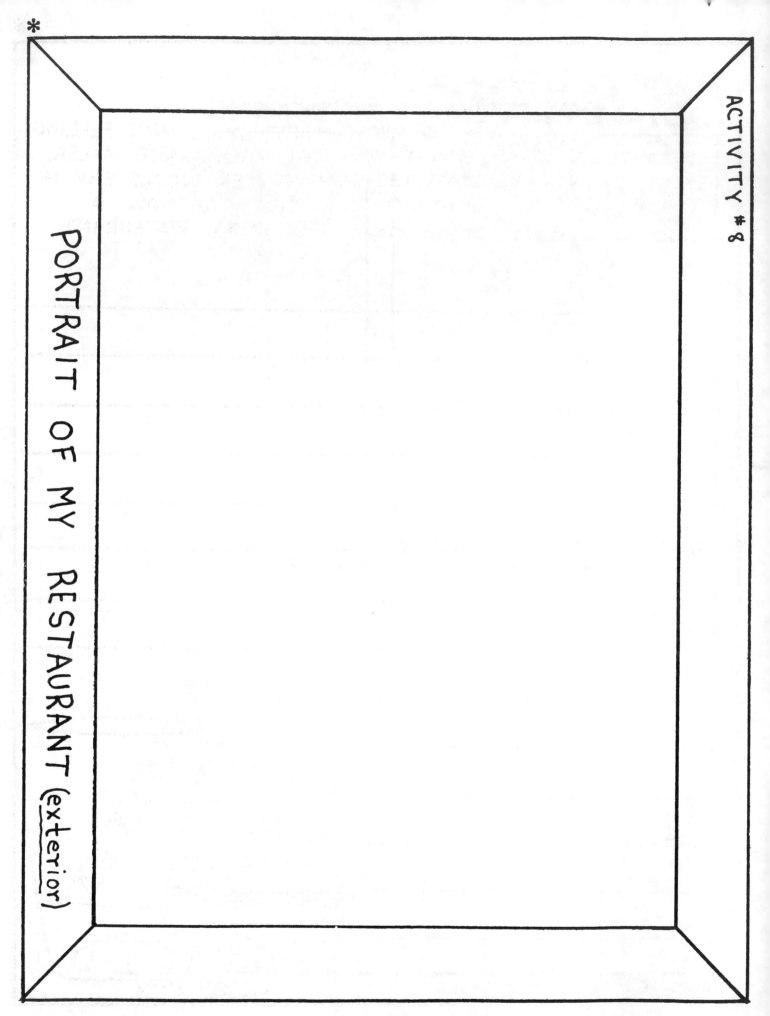

PORTRAIT OF MY RESTAURANT (exterior)

ACTIVITY #9

MANY THINGS IN MY RESTAURANT ARE INANIMATE ..... BUT I KNOW THEY STILL HAVE FEELINGS. SOMETIMES I THINK ABOUT HOW THE MILK SHAKE MAKER FEELS. I WONDER WHAT THE CASH REGISTER WOULD SAY IF IT COULD TALK. BELOW IS THE STORY OF HOW A _____ FEELS ABOUT LIFE IN MY RESTAURANT.

_____

_____

_____

_____

_____

_____

_____

_____

I'm proud to be a sesame seed.

_____

_____

I'm glad to be the last drop.

THERE IS MORE ON THE BACK

# ACTIVITY #10
# The Special of the House

OUR FAMOUS SPECIAL MOUTH-WATERING TREAT

Above: a picture of my famous food <u>creation</u>.

Below: the secret <u>recipe</u>. Just make and eat.

ACTIVITY #11

I have drawn a blueprint of my restaurant showing where the rooms, tables, doors, windows, etc. will be.

*

## ACTIVITY #12

Here is an advertisement I wrote for our radio station, WWKZ. I wrote a catchy jingle to make <u>potential</u> customers' taste buds tingle.

# HUNDREDS OF WAYS TO SAY WIN OR LOSE

Ed Sneed pads lead

## Robinson Spanks Cards

## Melton Returns To Haunt Sox, Angels Win, 10-5

QHS girls end Keokuk streak

Scott's Steal Sparks Celtics To Series Finale

Phillies' Quick Start Rips Astros

Kodes First-Round Tennis Victim

## Homers Key Dodgers Past Phillies, 8-4

Cubs' Zamora stops Cards

Blunt

## Fire sizzles 17-0

Cubs, Expos Rained Out

## USC Blasts Texas,

Player leads by five

Ashe, Dibbs Fall; Evert Still Winning

## Robinson's HR In 7th Lifts Bucs Past Cards, 2-1

Giants romp

Sox power

does it — barely

Tigers drop Kansas City

## Top Orioles not winging as high as in past

Blitz

The layout on the opposite page recreated on a piece of oaktag can easily serve as the focus point for a learning center. Have students bring in a variety of sports clippings from the newspaper. Cut off the headlines and glue them to the oaktag. Simply hang the completed replica of the opposite page on the wall or chalkboard and develop some ideas similar to those below and . . . Creative Writing in the center format. You may wish to establish some guides for using the center. One might be that a student must attempt three of the five activities. A second might say that by November 12 (or whatever date is appropriate) each student must have one activity in a polished form and must share it in some way with the rest of the class members.

ACTIVITY NO. 1    Study the sports headlines carefully. Pay special attention to the words that say whether a team or an individual won or lost. Words like: PAST, STOPS, THUMPS, LEADS, SPANKS, HAUNT, BLASTS, ROMP.

There must be hundreds of ways to say win or lose.

On a sheet of notebook paper make two lists. One list of all the words that can mean win. A second list of all the words that can mean lose.

ACTIVITY NO. 2    Now look over your two lists. Find your very best words. You will probably have several. Look your list over very carefully and choose your four or five best words.

With these words try writing some sports headlines. Experiment . . . try several. You should be able to create an exciting headline.

When you have your best headline . . . print it on a piece of white paper, in headline style. Then mount your headline on a piece of colored construction paper and hang it somewhere in the classroom.

ACTIVITY NO. 3    Now you are ready to look at all the various headlines your classmates have created. Study them carefully. Let the headlines turn on your imagination. Some headlines will help you to think of a lot of ideas. Choose the headline that motivates you most. Write a sports story to go with the headline.

ACTIVITY NO. 4    Here is something else you might like to try. Choose a headline from the list on the display board or choose a headline that you find in the paper that you think could be the title for a funny, imaginary sports story. For Example: GIANTS ROMP

New York City, NY . . . 4/16/79. Our local baseball boys had a very weird game last night. The tournament being held in Transylvania Park was turned into a playground when the opposing team turned up over 10 feet tall. Our local fighters were at first fearful of what the outcome of the game might be. Everyone believed that the Giant's would be able to hit the ball all the way to Detroit. As it turned out our local heroes had nothing to fear. True the Giants could hit hard, run fast, and throw straight. They were also too tall and could seldom stoop low enough to hit balls in the strike zone that were pitched by Tim Broderick. Final score Home Team 7 — Giants 3.

ACTIVITY NO. 5    Look at the sports stories on the blue card. You will find 10 of them. Read any five and write a headline for each.

Your students can make their own viewers and then .....

# CREATE

### their own

# FILMSTRIPS

**MATERIALS NEEDED:**

A styrofoam cup. (one per student)

A paper napkin. (the patterned ones are nice)

Some adding machine tape. (3 or 4 feet per student)

Polymer medium, or mod-podge, or a solution of half Elmer's glue and half water.

Some acrylic paints if you have them handy.

A small paint brush.

Some fine-tip felt markers. (variety of colors)

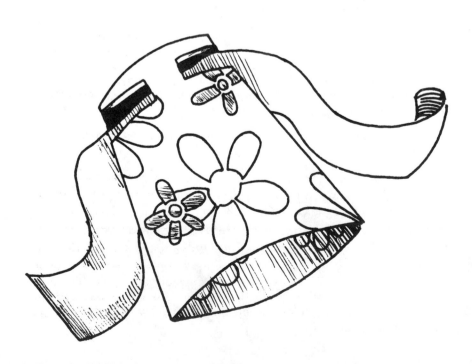

POOF!

THE END

# To Make the Viewer

1. Put a coat of polymer medium (or the mod-podge or Elmer's solution) on the styrofoam cup. Be careful to cover the entire surface, inside and outside.

2. Stick pieces or strips of the napkin down onto the inside/outside of the cup, covering the entire surface of the cup.

3. Now cover the cup with another coat of the polymer medium. The polymer and napkin strengthen and decorate the cup. If you have acrylic paints, you can decorate the cup . . . as soon as it dries.

4. When the cup is dry, it can also be decorated with the felt tip pens.

5. When the cup is completely decorated, cut two 1½ inch slits in it so that your filmstrip will thread and pull easily.

# Making the Filmstrips

1. Take the length of adding machine tape (talk nice and the school secretary may give you a roll) and cut it in half to a width of 1½ inches. This is your filmstrip.

2. Have the students use the various colors of felt-tip markers to write and draw their filmstrip.

3. Some students may choose to divide the filmstrip into frames to make it look more authentic.

4. When the filmstrip is completed, it is wise to cover both sides with clear contact paper. This, of course, makes it more durable, easier to thread and pull through the viewer.

Many of your students will enjoy making a wide variety of filmstrips for their viewers. Why not have them try this idea for a book report? It can be an excellent self-checking or testing device. First frame the question. Next frame the answer. Some students will enjoy writing and illustrating riddles this way. The possibilities are almost limitless.

Research shows that by the time the average person is 18 years old, he will have spent more time in front of a television set than in the classroom. Let's take advantage of this situation instead of fighting it. Students are turned on by television. The motivation is there. There relevance is also there . . . the students have a wealth of knowledge on which to build, because they have been involved with television since before they were one year old. Here are some ways to combine creative writing and television.

Watch any TV program of your choice and then write a one-paragraph summary of the program.

Happy Pup is a new dog food. Write a 30-second commercial advertising this product.

"Rhoda, Shirley, Maude and Mary Have Happy Times" is the name of a new series. Write and design the opening title and credits.

Try writing a couple of jokes for Johnny Carson's monologue.

Pretend you are the host of a variety show. Write introductions for 3 guests of your choice.

Watch the evening news on TV a couple of times. Write a 5-minute news program based on what's happening around school.

prospective girl friend. Keith: David Cassidy. Laurie: Susan Dey.

**44 LEAVE IT TO BEAVER** (BW)
Beaver panics when he loses a library book charged to his father. Beaver: Jerry Mathers.

**47 ZOOM—Children**

5:25 **7 WEATHER**

5:30 **3 8 ABC NEWS—Harry Reasoner**

**4 7 31 CBS NEWS—Cronkite**

**6 10 20 25 NBC NEWS—John Chancellor**

**9 BEWITCHED—Comedy**
Tabitha uses her bewitching talents to subdue a pesty playmate.

**12 ELECTRIC COMPANY—Children**

**19 NEWS**

**44 GOMER PYLE, USMC** (BW)
Carter, bound for a date, makes the mistake of giving Gomer a lift.

**47 CARRASCOLENDAS—Children**

### EVENING

6:00 **3 4 6 7 10 20 25 31 NEWS**

**8 BEVERLY HILLBILLIES**
A temporary but tempting Italian cook stirs up a storm. Jed: Buddy Ebsen. Granny: Irene Ryan.

**9 ANDY GRIFFITH—Comedy** (BW)
Fred Goss proposes to Aunt Bee. Fred: Fred Sherman.

**12 47 AVIATION WEATHER**

**19 TRUTH OR CONSEQUENCES**

**44 ROOM 222**
The throes of love are hard for Jason to handle. His new romance is filling his head with dreams of an early marriage, a step which could ruin his chances for a successful career as an artist. Jason: Heshimu. Amy: Dwan Smith. Pete: Lloyd Haynes.

6:25 **6 COMMENT**

6:30 **3 CANDID CAMERA**

**4 MATCH GAME PM**
Richard Dawson, Charles Nelson Reilly, Brett Somers, Bill Cullen, Janice Pennington and Fannie Flagg.

**6 HOLLYWOOD SQUARES—Game**
Robert Blake, Mac Davis, Phyllis Diller, Anthony Newley, Florence Henderson.

**7 BUGS BUNNY/ROAD RUNNER —Cartoon**
Daffy Duck appears as a Robin Hood who can't convince fat Friar Tuck (Porky Pig) of his identity in one of the program's four cartoons. Also: "The Abominable Snow Rabbit," starring Daffy and Bugs Bunny.

**8 ADAM-12—Crime Drama**
A do-gooder causes trouble for the officers with his efforts to transport a Christmas tree to an old-folks home. Malloy: Martin Milner.

**9 DICK VAN DYKE—Comedy** (BW)
Laura's and Rob's parents clash over the selection of cemetery plots. Rob: Dick Van Dyke.

**10 ADAM-12—Crime Drama**
Cases: a stolen-car ring, a liquor-store robbery and a child trapped in a refrigerator. Malloy: Martin Milner. Reed: Kent McCord. Owens: Timothy Brown.

**12 MARY JANE ODELL—Interview**

**19 HOGAN'S HEROES—Comedy**
Would you believe espionage in a hospital room? Dr. Klaus: Henry Corden. Hogan: Bob Crane. Klink: Werner Klemperer. Schultz: John Banner.

**20 WILD KINGDOM**
Remote-control, rocket-fired nets are used to capture the swift wildebeest and lion in a relocation project.

**25 ANDY GRIFFITH—Comedy**

Write a TV Guide to a typical day in your life. Try to program your daily schedule — from the time you get up (Good Morning, World) until you go to bed. Be sure all your friends, teachers, merchants are included in the capsule summaries. Be sure to include one close-up feature. Have fun! Be creative!

**close up**

MOVIE
8:00 **3 8 19**

### GAILY, GAILY

A small-town boy meets big-city slickers.

In this 1969 comedy, based on the cub-reporter days of playwright-screenwriter Ben Hecht ("The Front Page"), Beau Bridges gives a tongue-in-cheek performance as writer Ben Harvey, who arrives in Chicago in 1910 with high hopes of landing a job.

But Ben is soon down and out, the naive victim of pickpockets. Two unlikely benefactors, though, give him a fresh start: Queen Lil, the warmhearted madam of a bordello that Ben mistakes for a boardinghouse; and Francis X. Sullivan, the cynical, hard-drinking crime reporter who gives Ben a break on the paper—and a look at city life that puts an end to his wide-eyed innocence.

Music by Henry Mancini.

Supporting Cast . . . Lil: Melina Mercouri. Sullivan: Brian Keith. Adeline: Margot Kidder. Grogan: Hume Cronyn. Johanson: George Kennedy. Lilah: Melodie Johnson. Father: John Randolph. Governor: Wilfrid Hyde-White. (2 hrs.)

# Create Your Own TV Programs

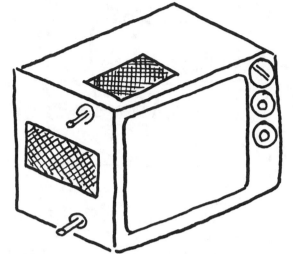

## How to Make:

### MATERIALS NEEDED —

A cardboard box
Rolls of white shelf paper
Writing/drawing instruments (pens, pencils, crayons, markers)
Stack of old magazines
Rubber cement
1 inch dowel rods or 2 old broom handles

### PUTTING IT TOGETHER —

Cut screen in front of box
Cut four holes for the ends of dowel rods to stick through . . . they should come out about 4 inches on each side
Cover box with wood grain contact paper
Add cardboard knobs and dials
Staple or tape ends of the shelf paper to the dowel rods.

### MORE HINTS —

Students can cut and glue not only pictures from the magazines but also words.
Rubber cement will not wrinkle the paper the way white glue will.
Sometimes stories roll better if one turner is on each side of the box turning at the same time.
This can be a good group activity. Allow students to work in groups of 3 or 4 to create their TV stories.

Create a program about your school ...... your community ...... your state ....... Write a travelogue on each of our 50 states ..... Create a segment of As The World Turns or Mary Hartman... ... teach a basic skill as on Sesame Street .... don't forget book reports .... Each student can write his/her autobiography..... or create a new TV series.

CREATIVE WRITING

for a big wall

OUR CLASS

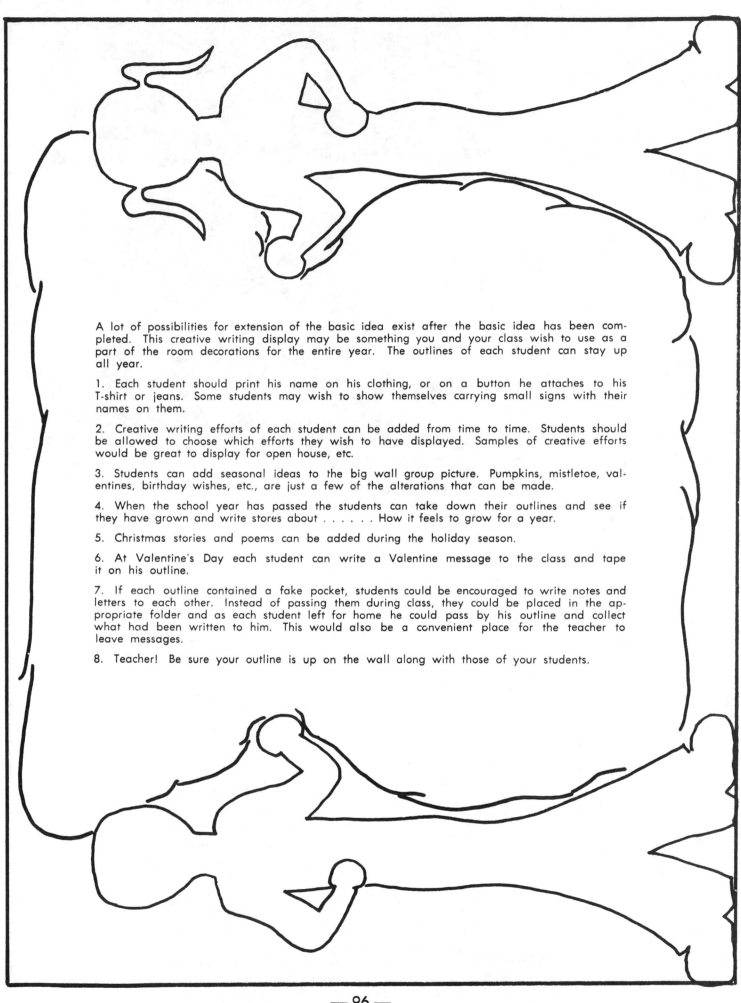

A lot of possibilities for extension of the basic idea exist after the basic idea has been completed. This creative writing display may be something you and your class wish to use as a part of the room decorations for the entire year. The outlines of each student can stay up all year.

1. Each student should print his name on his clothing, or on a button he attaches to his T-shirt or jeans. Some students may wish to show themselves carrying small signs with their names on them.

2. Creative writing efforts of each student can be added from time to time. Students should be allowed to choose which efforts they wish to have displayed. Samples of creative efforts would be great to display for open house, etc.

3. Students can add seasonal ideas to the big wall group picture. Pumpkins, mistletoe, valentines, birthday wishes, etc., are just a few of the alterations that can be made.

4. When the school year has passed the students can take down their outlines and see if they have grown and write stores about . . . . . . How it feels to grow for a year.

5. Christmas stories and poems can be added during the holiday season.

6. At Valentine's Day each student can write a Valentine message to the class and tape it on his outline.

7. If each outline contained a fake pocket, students could be encouraged to write notes and letters to each other. Instead of passing them during class, they could be placed in the appropriate folder and as each student left for home he could pass by his outline and collect what had been written to him. This would also be a convenient place for the teacher to leave messages.

8. Teacher! Be sure your outline is up on the wall along with those of your students.

# CEREAL BOX WRITING

Begin saving empty cereal boxes. Save large ones and save small ones. Involve your students in the saving effort. You will need these to use as the focus of this CREATIVE WRITING CENTER.

The tasks you design for your "CEREAL CENTER" can range from simple to involved. But all the activities should require that the student be fluent, flexible, original, or elaborative in his thinking.

MATERIALS NEEDED:

........... a work table shoved against a wall or into a corner of your room.

........... lots of cereal boxes — large and small.

........... a stack of writing paper.

........... a stack of construction paper of various colors.

........... a stack of old magazines.

........... pencils, pens, markers, scissors, glue.

........... chairs around the open sides of table.

........... one cereal box covered with bright contact paper and labeled COMPLETED WORK.

........... a large sheet of paper covering the wall behind the work table with the directions and activities printed on it.

# POSSIBLE ACTIVITIES

1. Make a list of possible names for a new cereal. Then choose your best name and choose one of the empty cereal boxes and design the box. Be sure to write all information on all sides. You may use any of the materials you find on this table.

2. You may have one cup of "Alpha-Bits." Dip in and pour out the pieces and use them to write a note, poem, or letter. Just glue them on a piece of dark construction paper.

3. Write a new television commercial for a cereal. It can be an existing cereal or a new brand that you invent. When you finish make a final copy in your best handwriting, mount it on a piece of construction paper and tape it to the wall behind the work table.

4. Imagine you fell asleep and woke up to find that you had changed into a Rice Krispy and are inside a fresh box on the grocer's shelf. Write your life story.

5. Pick a cereal — perhaps your favorite — find out how it is made. What are the ingredients? What company makes it? Write to the company and ask for all the information they can send you. See what you can find out about the history of the cereal. When all information is in, write a report that you will read to the class.

6. Mix up the names of familiar cereals — at least 20 that you know of. For example: Corn Flakes = CRON SKALFE. When your list is completed give it to a friend and allow him to try to unscramble your efforts.

These six creative writing ideas can be written on the side of a large empty cereal box. Directions could be: Each student must do three out of these six ideas.

SEND FOR FREE
NAME
ADDRESS
CITY
STATE
ZIP

12 OZ. NT.W
A FULL BOX
MUST ALLO
FOR SET
WHILE
CONTEN
THIS P
ARE
FRO
TO
H

Group project. Students can work in groups of four to develop a campaign to get their cereal elected . . . CEREAL OF THE YEAR. Posters must be made. A campaign slogan must be adopted. A newspaper advertisement must be designed. Campaign buttons mut be created. A letter for a mass mailing to all the voters must be written. When all work is completed hold a school assembly. Have a parade of the nominated cereals. Put up the posters throughout the school. Pass out the buttons and letters. Give the written speeches. Hold the election during the assembly and crown the CEREAL OF THE YEAR.

**SMOKIE**

Turn a refrigerator box into a giant cereal box. Make it as detailed as possible. Put a door in it so students can go inside and become the cereal. Students could be a raisin from raisin bran, one fiber from a loaf of shredded wheat, or a piece of coconut from granola. When each student emerges from the box he must write down thoughts about how it would feel to be a piece of cereal. To further create a cereal climate in the giant box, tape record the sounds of cereal being poured, eaten, crunched, etc. Students can play this recording while they are sitting inside the box. You might even place a box of cereal inside to munch on while sitting and thinking.

ED DRY ART. CORN, 100% VITAMINS WHO ARTIFICIAL WHEAT, ROASTED SWEE, BARLE FREE SWEETNER FROM TINER

**NEW IMPROVED — MORE NUTRITION**

**CORN**

**OATS QUAKER**

For another center activity, name as many cereals as you have students in your class. Place these names in an empty cereal box. Tape a 3" x 5" index card to the outside of the box with the following directions: Reach in and without looking choose one slip of paper. This slip will have the name of a cereal on it. You are to design a page for our GUIDE TO CEREALS BOOKLET. Your page will concern the cereal you have just drawn. Each page in the book will be on a sheet of white duplicating paper. When you finish, your page should inform the readers of the guide as much as possible about your cereal.

Another center activity could be:

Into several variety-pack size cereal boxes, place slips of paper. Each slip of paper should contain a task. Tasks could include:

1. Write a poem about me.
2. Make a list of all the words that rhyme with me.
3. How many smaller words can you make from my name.
4. Write a riddle about me.
5. Make a list of all the possible ways that I can be improved so that more people will purchase me.
6. Alphabetize the names of all the cereals you can think of.
7. Write a recipe using me as one of the basic ingredients.
8. Write down directions for fixing a bowl of me. The person who reads these directions has never seen or heard of cereal before.

**Build A Portable Creative Writing Gallery**

## YOU WILL NEED:

- 10  1'' x 3'' pine strips. Each strip should be 6' long. Paint these black.
- 5  2' x 4' masonite panels. Each should be painted a bright color.
- 6  small hinges (like for doors)
- 36  wood screws

Screw 2 strips to each panel as shown. Hinge 2 panels together for one section of the gallery and hinge the other 3 panels together for the second section. The gallery can now be folded flat and transported easily in a station wagon. It can also be arranged in several different ways.

Now you have a great way to display your student creative writing efforts. They will be proud of the creative writing gallery. Both sides can be used so there will be ample space.

From time to time you may wish to place creative writing assignments on some sections of the gallery. It is also a good place for motivating pictures. By folding the 3-section-piece you can create a creative writing corner.

Your creative writing gallery will be a great showcase for open house, seasonal celebrations, etc. It can be used in the classroom, in the hall and in the learning center or at the entrance to the school building.

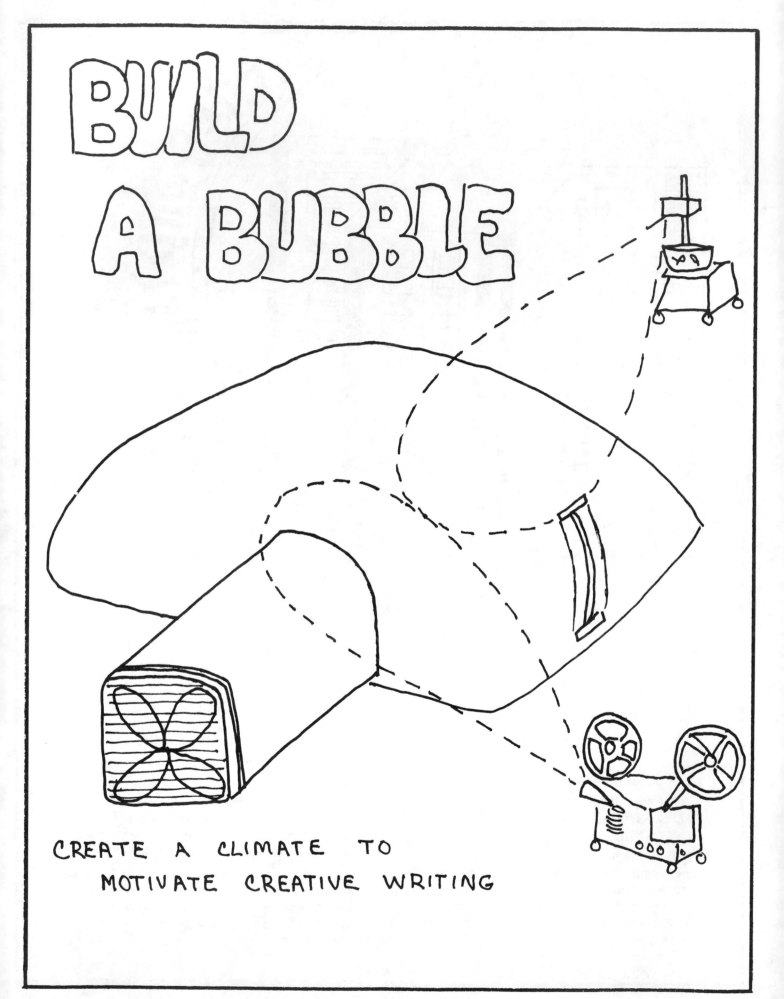

# BUILD A BUBBLE

CREATE A CLIMATE TO
MOTIVATE CREATIVE WRITING

MATERIALS NEEDED:

    4 mil polyurethane plastic (visqueene) from a lumber yard
    2 inch ''duck'' tape or clear plastic tape from a sporting goods store
    1 portable window fan

CONSTRUCTION:

    To build a simple bubble shape cut a sheet of plastic 12' x 24'.
    Fold it in half to form a square 12' x 12'.
    Use tape to seal the three open sides.
    Make a tube to fit around your fan, cut slit in bubble and attach fan and
        tube.
    Now inflate.
    Cut vertical slit for door and reinforce with tape.
    Your bubble is built . . . quick and easy.
    It will inflate and deflate in just a few seconds.

You have now built a multisensory, inflatable environment that will set your imagination free. It can really be built any shape . . . any size. You can create any place on earth or beyond by projecting images on its surface. Inside you will be completely surrounded by color, motion, visual images and sound.

Create the bottom of the sea with films of the sea focused on the bubble. Place blue acetate on overhead projector and then place a glass bowl with 6-8 goldfish in it on the stage. Focus these on the bubble. Hang blue and green streamers inside and cover the floor with foam cushions or balloons, and presto . . . in a darkened room you are on the bottom of the sea.

Just think of the motivation you have provided for a variety of creative writing activities . . . poems, short stories, how it feels to deep-sea dive, what does a fish feel,etc.

In addition, play sea music on the record player. Film loops of sea life can also add to the atmosphere. The bubble can be set up in the corner of your classroom, the schools learning center, the stage or the gym. Your students can write a tour-guide script and invite other classrooms of children to enjoy the experience.

OTHER BUBBLE IDEAS:

Learn and write about light from inside a lightbulb. Use the colors of the rainbow or prisms. Construct a bubble in a lightbulb shape. Have students write about how it feels to glow, or about being electricity.

On a nice spring day take your bubble outside and place it under a sprinkler or spray it with a garden hose. Students can write about being inside a raindrop.

The possibilities are almost endless.

WHAT

WHO

WHEN

WHERE

## WHO !  WHAT !  WHEN !  WHERE !

Sometimes students have trouble knowing what to write about. One solution can be a set of Who, What, When, and Where dials. Sometimes, because it is easier, teachers have all students write on the same topic. Somehow this does not seem fair . . . at least not all the time. The solution for the busy teacher is a set of Who, What, When, and Where dials.

Just spin each dial. Collect the information that the arrows point to and a prospective writer has the basic ingredients for a story. Even for those times when everyone writes on the same topic the Who, What, When, and Where dials can be used. It just takes one second to spin. It might be wise to allow some group discussion before writing begins.

The dials can be made from pizza wheels. Find the center of the pizza wheel, and divide the surface into sections. Use bright, colorful magic markers or crayons to write the possibilities in the various sections . A spinner can be made from most any kind of stiff paper. Punch a hole, with a nail in the center of the pizza wheel. Place a thin washer over the hole. On top of that place the cardboard spinner. Next punch a hole in the spinner. Thread a brad through. Bend and tape the ends of the brad to the backside of the pizza wheel and one of your dials is ready to be used.

If you cannot get pizza wheels just glue together two circles made from poster board. When you have completed your dial, you may wish to cover it with clear contact paper to make it last longer.

To increase the plots, you may wish to create additional dials. Doing this will also provide for variation. Each student must use the indicated ideas from four out of five of the dials. Add additional variation by having all students use the same who but a what based on their own spin.

Ideas for a WHY dial

mother said so
because I just had to
a bully forced me to
I was hypnotized
held at gunpoint
fear overcame me
I had to go to the bathroom
because I deserved it
I was bad
the devil made me do it
everyone else did it

Ideas for a HOW dial

very, very carefully
quickly and quietly
through my inventiveness
with the help of my friends
slowly and silently
under pressure
entirely by myself
without any tools
in a state of shock
with $1,000,000.01

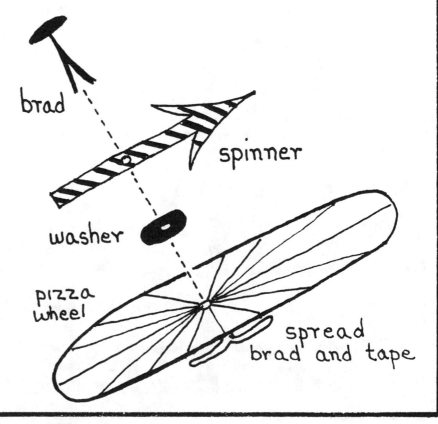

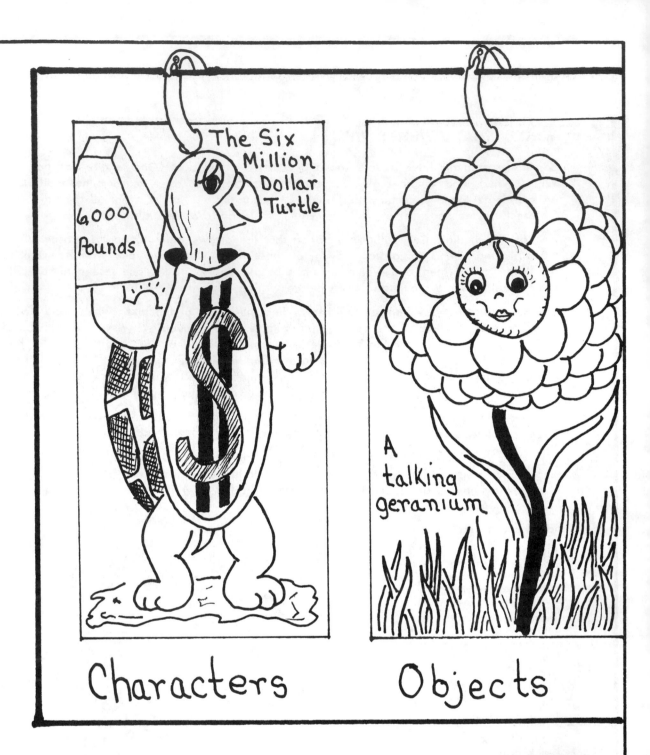

Characters

Objects

# FLIP·A·PLOT
## FOR
## CREATIVE WRITING

Aboard a UFO

Butterflies by the millions

## Where

## Conditions

### MATERIALS NEEDED

2 pieces of posterboard (24'' x 12'') . . . glue these together and cover with a bright solid contact paper.

40 - 60 squares of poster board each 6'' x 10''. Each square will serve as a plot card.

Use a paper punch and metal rings to attach the plot cards to the baseboard.

### TO USE:

On any table or an empty desk just place the ''FLIP-A-PLOT'' and some paper and pencils. Now you have 100's of possible plots and the materials for a creative writing center.

You can draw the various plot cards or find pictures in magazines (cut out and glue). Old textbooks, dime store story books, and greeting cards are also good sources for pictures. Photographs of your students can also be used. As you find new pictures make and add new cards.

# Directions:

Flip through the various plot cards in each of the four stacks. Maybe even close your eyes and let your imagination soar. Then after you have looked through and imagined . . . . . . MAKE A DECISION . . . . . Decide on one card from each of the stacks. These 4 ideas you have chosen can develop into your creative writing effort for the day or week.

# Plot Possibilities:

## CHARACTERS

the handsome prince
Mother Nature
Super Chicken
The Old Woman Who Lived in a Shoe
the butler
the Cookie Monster
a green giraffe
several Bunching Bananas
Donnie and Marie Osmond
the Man from Glad

## OBJECTS

an electric skateboard
a speeding locomotive
a magic apple
an 80-foot yellow ribbon
a bionic arm
a talking geranium
the Statue of Liberty melting
the ultra secret
a clock that hums
a 100-pound football
ten gold-plated whistles

## WHERE

at the White House
on a run-away reindeer
on a dersticle
aboard a UFO
floating on a pink cloud
your 85th birthday party
on a magical mystery tour
riding a falling star
locked in the school at night

## OTHER CONDITIONS

it's raining cats and dogs
butterflies by the millions
1,000 pounds of butter melting
an erupting volcano
an airplane without a pilot
in the middle of the night
boxes and boxes of soda bottle caps
a crackling fire
falling and falling and falling